A RECIPE FOR COOKING

ALSO BY CAL PETERNELL
Twelve Recipes

A RECIPE FOR COOKING

CAL PETERNELL

𝒲𝓂
WILLIAM MORROW
An Imprint of HarperCollinsPublishers

HarperCollins books may be purchased for educational, business, or sales promotional use. For information please e-mail the Special Markets Department at SPsales@harpercollins.com.

FIRST EDITION

Designed by Suet Yee Chong
Photographs by Ed Anderson / Styling by George Dolese
Illustrations by Liam Peternell, Milo Henderson, Henderson Peternell,
Kathleen Henderson, and Cal Peternell
Cover illustration by Kathleen Henderson

Library of Congress Cataloging-in-Publication Data has been applied for.

ISBN 978-0-06-242786-1

16 17 18 19 20   ID/RRD   10 9 8 7 6 5 4 3 2 1

For Kathleen—everything I cook,
everything I do, is more delicious with you

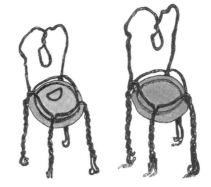

CONTENTS

All Up in a Cabbage Leaf | Yogurt-Fried Black Pepper Chicken | Turkey Breast Scaloppine Grilled with Herbs: A Rallying Cry | Duck Cooked Two Ways | Lamb Shoulder Braised with Moroccan Spices and Green Olives | Spicy Ground Pork with Ginger, Lime, Peppers, and Green Beans | Pork Belly Braised with Fennel Seeds and Sweet Wine | Rolled Pork Loin Roast Stuffed with Olives and Herbs | Cast-Iron Pan Roast | Braised and Grilled or Griddled Short Ribs

FOREWORD

Hello, Fellow Lover of Food. My name is Chris, and I
do not know how to cook.

During what would otherwise have been my college/getting-so-sick-
of-Top-Ramen-that-you-start-doing-something-about-it years, I was on
tour with a band I cofounded called Nickel Creek. Days off and hotel
rooms with kitchenettes almost never coincided. Days off and restaurants
owned by buddies of concert promoters, on the other hand . . .

So I never learned how to cook, but boy did I ever learn how to eat! I
would spend every minute that wasn't earmarked for music-making fig-
uring out how to put my bandmates and myself in the way of the absolute
best dinners possible, and those dinners ended up sustaining us in ways
that went far beyond physical nourishment. They gave us a chance to
catch our breath, to relate to each other as people (not just musicians),
and to develop a strong sense of community despite our nomadic exis-
tence . . . *and* they were fun as hell.

But when I arrived back home after a month or two of that, rather
than boldly head for the kitchen to see if I could stumble into a passable
re-creation of any of the incredible food I'd just eaten, I would go right
back out my front door to see how my local restaurants were stacking up
to the cream of the past tour's crop. That was my relationship with food:

a long series of lovely one-night stands. Until I started hanging out with a fellow named Mike Marshall.

Mike knows how to play *and* cook. I spent a week making a record with him at his place in Oakland, California, and it changed my entire outlook on the nature of eating. I'd been using food as a means of escape from/reward for withstanding the cares of the day, whereas Mike saw it and those very same cares as mutually beautifying strands to be woven into the fabric of a good day. As I look back, it's impossible to say exactly when or how the meals and music would begin or end. I'd wake up, drag my mandolin out to the kitchen (perhaps to make sure I could remember something we'd come up with the night before and not properly documented . . . ah, wine!), and find Mike pouring old-school stovetop espresso, cutting biscotti fresh out of the oven, and grabbing *his* mandolin to join in on the hunt for last night's idea. And as if by magic, fresh fruit and an omelet would appear—but we would also find the missing idea, and wait, whoa, there's *that* song written, and are we actually having the best smoked chicken salad on earth for lunch now? Hard to tell because we're also about to finish recording that song on the wings of the last round of espresso and a square of dark chocolate while rolling pasta dough, washing the chanterelles we foraged earlier (?!?), and discussing each other's relationships over an early evening glass of *hot damn, Mikey, this is the life!!!* To which he would invariably reply, "Dude, this is nothing. You gotta hang with my buddy Cal."

And hang with his buddy, Cal Peternell, I did. I suspect if you've gotten this far, Fellow Lover of Food, you know at least a little about Cal's subtle but rampant badassery. The first thing I noticed about him was that he was *listening*. Listening in a rare, wonderful way to everyone and everything: his guests (in this case, Mike and me), his beautiful family, the pans on the stove, the vegetables under his knife, the record playing in the background . . . listening as if every sound were part of a recipe for a beautiful evening with which the universe had entrusted us. The next thing I noticed was his selfless virtuosity. Virtuosity for its own sake (I think of the last tower of molecular gastronomy I dared raise my fork against, or Paganini's twenty-four death-defying caprices) can be thrilling, but only rarely transcendent. True virtuosi place their technical accomplishment at the service of their imaginations *and* the imaginations of their collaborators and audience. If you've ever listened to Glenn Gould play Bach's Goldberg Variations, or dined at Chez Panisse during Cal's tenure as head chef, you know exactly what I'm talking about. That inaugural feast was a brilliant, unhurried, graceful fantasia, both composed and improvised, for kitchen, living room, dining room, and seven people.

I mean, I still heartily disagree with Mike's humble assessment of his own formidable cooking and hospitality chops, but can confirm just as heartily that Cal is a bona fide master. All subsequent meals over the last ten-plus years, whether at Chez Panisse or Chez Someone We Know, have been equally revelatory. A multi-part exploration/celebration of the good things life has to offer, and of the fact that though human beings are the absolute worst in myriad ways, we're also uniquely capable of extracting beauty and meaning from just about anything.

And so, Fellow Lover of Food, I wish you great joy in your pursuit of the most beautiful mornings, afternoons, and evenings imaginable, with this book as a guide. Actually, you know what? I'm gonna join you. I may not know how to cook, but my buddy Cal just gave me the recipe!

Chris Thile
Portland, Oregon (but probably somewhere else when you read this)
2016

INTRODUCTION

I remember the day my professional cooking life changed, the day it started to make sense with the rest of my life and not seem like it was time for a new career. We were out food shopping, and my wife, Kathleen, had parked across from the cheese shop and right in front of Chez Panisse.

"You can't park here," I told her. "It's a yellow curb."

"I'm not parking, I'm dropping you off. You should work here; this is the right place for you. Go in, they'll hire you, you're great."

"But I already have a job, and . . . me? At *Chez Panisse*!?" I said to the back of the car as my pregnant wife and our three-year-old son pulled away. Then, I turned and went in and got myself hired at an amazing restaurant, the kind that keeps cooks around and allows them to mature both in and out of the kitchen.

Kathleen was right that day, and twenty years and two sons later, the place still inspires me and encourages me to inspire others—not just guests and cooks, but my sons as well. I've taught them a lot, and though they know the basics of eating and cooking well, lately I was sensing that they seemed ready for more. Or some of the time they did. My second son, Milo, born the year I started working at Chez Panisse, will still throw down like lots of other kids, cooking up bagel melts or quesadillas, bean dip or poached eggs for his little brother, Liam. But there's also interest in some serious cooking, real sauces, homemade pasta or pizza, exotic ingredients and complex preparations. Henderson, my eldest, cooked his way through art school in New York, spending mornings stretching canvases and mixing colors and evenings rolling pasta, composing salads, and stirring sauces at some first-class restaurants. He, and Milo, have done stints in the kitchens and dining rooms at Chez Panisse, and even young Liam helps pop favas from their skins after school, wondering aloud who came up with a bean that has to be peeled twice.

"And who even likes them?" he marvels.

From opening cans into skillets to separating eggs for soufflés, we do many types of cooking. They share a simple aim—getting ourselves fed—but how we cook and how we eat can vary widely and depend on a complex equation whose factors include appetite, time, funds, ingredients, and motivation. When the equation adds up in a way that allows for it, we might take some time, allow our minds and skillets to wander, and find that is where the fun can be. In the same way that a taco eaten at the truck in the parking lot can be every bit as satisfying as a sit-down, multi-course, fancy restaurant dinner, the quickest, humblest meal made at home can be just as good as the most involved and luxurious one. There are the meals for when time is short, when eggs are easy enough to boil and halve and set alongside a fresh leafy salad, warm roasted vegetables, or a ladleful of beans for a fine home-cooked meal with minimal cleanup. I love the simple pastas, curries, and soups that many of us survive on and can put quickly together on weeknights and that, when combined with excellent tablemates, reliably make good food into great meals.

But sometimes we're inspired to do a little more, and sometimes, a lot more. Deciding wisely when to cook what is essential for remaining in the comfortable context of your life, while still eating well. Maintaining that balance can be tricky—hunger, housework, homework, overtime, and simply not enough time can knock a cook out of whack and into frustration.

Fortunately, there is a recipe for cooking. Unwritten, perhaps, and not a recipe for a single dish, but for cooking itself. It is not fixed, and the variations are numberless. The ingredient list includes not only the foodstuffs and equipment available, your skill level, budget, and friends to help clean up, but also—especially—the amount of time you're able to put in. An occasion can change the cooking recipe a bit—maybe you'll add a dash more time, toss in a handful of family helpers, push some skill level limits, and crack, if not break, the budget. A birthday, a holiday, a dinner with old and new friends, or just a couple of quiet days ahead of you, and going all out, or mostly out, starts the wheels turning and mouth watering. Maybe marinating a big cut of meat to grill or roast is in order, or seasoning a pork shoulder or some duck legs for braising up sweet and tender the next day. Something impressive and delicious that you can start today and finish tomorrow and will, overnight, quietly impart a sense of well-being, of multitasking acumen. Maybe you'll even make dessert and maybe, like me, you have kids who are eager(ish) to help with project-oriented cooking like this. Especially with the dessert.

This is a cookbook for when you want to cook more than what's just necessary, for when you want to do some plotting and planning, plenty of stirring and peeling, and a measure of fretting over the little things. It's not only about cooking for groups—a dinner for two can involve every bit as much thought and effort as a holiday feast—but it *is* always for when we want to steer our cooking in a direction farther than simply bellyward. These are recipes for meals to put together when the cooking's the thing: for when we have good friends to laugh, drink, and cook with, or for when we want to dig deep into recipes and spend some quiet kitchen hours collecting ourselves by slicing, seasoning, and simmering. Dinners to make introductions, to commemorate, to celebrate, even, on occasion, to gently instigate. Lunches, too, the kind that last, with plenty of cold wine, lazily served courses, and plans for naps or long walks before dinner. These meals needn't be expensive. Forethought really helps, but you needn't be bound by it. Conviction and a positive spirit, though they may ebb and flow, are necessary.

These are recipes from home, but because there is really no way to disentangle the way I cook at home and what we do at Chez Panisse, this book constitutes a blending of two kitchens, uniting the generosity and warmth of home with the integrity and focus of work. There is a commonality that makes kitchens a sort of public space, no matter where they are. We make them our own, but we don't own them, nor would we want to—kitchens are for sharing: sharing food, sharing stories, and sharing counter space. The kitchen is the room where transformations of substance happen and where a material contact with the world outside is made. Regardless of where you bought it, your sustenance came from a patch of dirt on a farm, and it entered your home, as a friend would, through the kitchen door.

Good meals often yield good stories, and stories, on my list of life's essentials, are right up there with food, air, and love. We need stories because they are how we know who we are, and who we were. And because stories told about food have the power to evoke especially keen memories, I keep a diary of meals, inconsistently—a little ragged journal, oil-spotted from time in the kitchen counter jumble. It's not a record of every meal, and not just the special event meals—there are many very humble entries. But each of them conjures a moment, an evening, the characters, and the food. They are meals that tell stories about friends telling stories around a table, talking about their kids and their lives. My journal recalls the sounds and smells of cooking, and the food tells in turn the stories of farmers and fishermen and ranchers. For me these are recollections every bit as evocative as the photos that are effortlessly and endlessly snapped, if not more so—the written record, rewarding to make, delivers memories more satisfying and colorful than the gray glow of the ubiquitous two-by-three screen.

There is a story I like from a kids' book. It's about a lazy-seeming mouse named Frederick who, while his family collects seeds and berries for the long winter, collects the colors of summer. As the others roll pinecones and corncobs into the nest, Frederick carefully saves words, poems, and stories for when the food runs out and spirits run low. As they toil away, his family questions the value of Frederick's work and whether, indeed, it is work at all. Later, when the last acorn is eaten and the world has yet to defrost, dispirited, cold, and hungry, the mice turn to Frederick, and in the end, his stories are the nourishment they need to make it through until spring. They survive on tales of hope, the kind that lift us out of darkness and turn us from our darker selves, back into the sunlight.

What isn't a part of Leo Lionni's wonderful book, but that I often wonder about, is this: Just what sort of corn was it? How were the acorns stored and prepared, and did the pinecones have nuts in them? Did they dry some of the berries or eat them all first, fresh, with juicy little whiskers? And although it is true that Frederick's hard work, his faithfully remembered renderings of warmth and light, certainly does save them all, haven't the others kept *him* alive as well? Maybe they've done more than just keep Frederick alive. Maybe they put some love and attention into that little mouse kitchen, and then sat and ate, all of them together, and got the sort of sustenance that allows for inspiration to happen.

May this book embolden you in the kitchen, inspire you to find good ingredients, and enable you to cook them with confidence and pleasure. And when the eating is done, I hope that you'll have great stories to tell and fond listeners with stories of their own.

GENERAL NOTES ON COOKING

Some of the recipes in this book are complex and include grace notes that I hope will make them captivating and memorable, but if graceful complexity is more than you're up to tonight, parts can often be omitted without losing the charm. Similarly, first courses can be made a bit bigger for times when the first course will also be the last because, phew, what a day! I urge you to get into the kitchen but not to disappear into it. Do what is right for tonight and everyone will be happier.

Whether you're cooking a recipe from a cookbook that you've never tried before, or whipping up your signature classic, it is essential to taste, taste, and taste. Most ingredients can and should be tasted raw so that you know what you're working with; tasting is the most reliable and accurate way of determining doneness; and, for foods that need cooking before they can be properly tasted, you can make a mini version (one or two ravioli, a tiny fishcake, a nugget of sausage, and so on), cook it, taste it, and apply changes to the whole batch. Paying attention to what you learn from careful tasting is the single most important skill in the kitchen.

Cooking is easier when you don't have to start from scratch every time, and that means establishing a pantry of staples (and creating and using leftovers strategically). Everyone has their own version; here's what I keep in mine:

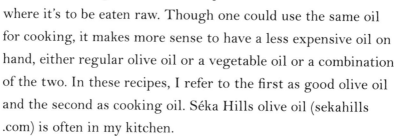

Fine sea salt (kosher salt is acceptable, table salt is not) and a loaded peppermill

Oils: I use my best-tasting extra-virgin olive oil in vinaigrettes and other places where it's to be eaten raw. Though one could use the same oil for cooking, it makes more sense to have a less expensive oil on hand, either regular olive oil or a vegetable oil or a combination of the two. In these recipes, I refer to the first as good olive oil and the second as cooking oil. Séka Hills olive oil (sekahills .com) is often in my kitchen.

I like to have a quart or two of grapeseed or rice bran oil on hand for deep-frying as well.

Red wine vinegar, champagne or white wine vinegar, sherry vinegar, cider vinegar, and balsamic vinegar

All-purpose flour, 00 flour, whole wheat flour, rye flour, rice flour, and chickpea flour

Cornmeal and polenta

Brown and white basmati rice, short-grained rice such as Carnaroli

Baking supplies, including sugars, baking powder and soda, vanilla extract, cocoa powder

Dried beans, chickpeas, and lentils

Whole spices (The aromatic quality of spices is multiplied if they are toasted and ground right before using. To accomplish this, heat a small skillet to medium and add the seeds. When they start to hop around a little and smell spicy, shake the pan and toast for 15 seconds. Tip them into a mortar or spice mill and grind as fine or coarse as you like.)

Almonds, walnuts, hazelnuts, pistachios, or pine nuts (To toast: Heat the oven to 350°F. Put the nuts on a baking sheet and into the oven for 8 minutes. Cut one in half to check if it's done—it should be tan inside. If it's still pale, reset the timer for 3 minutes and put the nuts back in. Repeat until done, then let the nuts cool before you chop them, if that's what's needed. Pine nuts are small enough that they can also be toasted in a skillet over low heat, shaken frequently.)

Cans of anchovies, whole tomatoes, and, just in case, beans

Olives and salt-packed capers (The flavor of salt-packed capers is superior to that of brined, but they must be very well soaked or they're way too salty. Cover them generously with warm water for at least an hour, changing the water several times. Taste, and soak some more if needed.)

When you are sautéing or pan-frying in a skillet, especially over high heat, the pan should be dry, without oil, until it's hot and ready for cooking. The oil should be added only then, and the food you are cooking should follow quickly and carefully. Overheated oil tastes burned and can make everything else taste that way, too.

For recipes that call for grilling, here are some technique guidelines:

> Gas grills are convenient, but I prefer to grill over wood charcoal. Light charcoal with natural fire-starters or with newspaper in a chimney device.

> Grill only over hot coals, never over flames—the soot they produce makes food taste bad.

> When the coals are ready and the grill grates are hot, they need to be well cleaned. I use a wire brush to scrub the grates till all the burned gunk is off, and then wipe them down with paper towels or wads of newspaper till they come up clean. A quick swipe with an oiled paper is a good finish. The notion that not cleaning the grate—that all that burned stuff gives good grilled flavor—is bunk.

> Vegetables, meats, poultry, and fish should all be at room temperature, seasoned with salt and pepper, and lightly coated with oil before hitting the hot grill.

Many recipes call for raw garlic pounded with a pinch of salt, which reduces the garlic to an almost liquid mash. I do this with a mortar and pestle or on a cutting board with the side of a chef's knife, crushing and mincing till it says uncle.

In recent years, I have made better friends with my freezer, especially for meats. When frozen and defrosted properly, meats from the freezer cook up fine, and taste just as good, in fact, as fresh. And for small farmers with relatively small groups of animals ready for slaughter each week, this is important. Freezing meats allows them to wait and take larger numbers less often. They sell some fresh right away and freeze the rest to sell over the next month or so, until the next harvest. Support these small farms, buy the frozen meats, and always defrost in the refrigerator, not at room temperature, for best results.

Meats that are to be braised or made into confit should be seasoned the day before, refrigerated, and brought to room temperature before cooking. If you forgot, season and leave them at room temperature for at least an hour, and next time don't forget.

APERITIVI:
BEFORE THE BEGINNING

Whether called hors d'oeuvres, aperitifs, aperitivi, meze, appetizers, starters, or snacks, it means the same thing: tasty bites that are served so everyone can just relax while you take your sweet time making a wonderful dinner. It can be a bowl of olives or nuts or radishes, super simple, or as cleverly complex as you want to get. If you're feeling it, this is where you can really go all out—these little bites are to have with drinks, and you don't need a lot, so . . . salty, spicy, hot, chilled, fatty, expensive even . . . all are good. The only rule—and it applies to professional and amateur alike—is that they have to be completely ready, or very nearly, so as not to lose the delicious-distraction advantage that a good platter of hors d'oeuvres, aperitifs, aperitivi, meze, appetizers, starters, or snacks can provide a cook deep in the midst of it.

OLIVES WITH CITRUS ZESTS AND FRIED HERBS

If I were your menu handicapper and you were looking for a sure thing, well, I got the horse right here. These shiny, festive olives are straightforward, look impressive, and will run for days. Can do, can do.

Makes 3 cups

1 orange

1 lemon

3 tablespoons good olive oil

20 sage leaves, picked from the stems

20 rosemary leaves, picked from the stems

1 small garlic clove, skin left on, cracked

1 pound favorite olives (a mix, say, of black Niçoise with green Lucques or Castelvetrano)

Crushed red pepper flakes

With a vegetable peeler, take 5 or 6 big strips of zest from the orange and lemon and set aside.

Heat a skillet or saucepan to medium. Add the oil, herbs, and garlic, and when the leaves have nearly stopped sizzling, about 20 seconds, turn off the heat and add the olives, citrus zests, and red pepper flakes. Turn everything out into a bowl and grate the remaining zest from the orange and lemon over the olives for extra flavor. Stir well and eat them warm or cool. If you don't eat all the olives now, discard the garlic, then save the rest in the refrigerator.

PISTACHIOS OR ALMONDS TOASTED WITH SAFFRON AND LEMON

My friend Samin rarely travels to her home country of Iran, but when she does, she brings back exotics like inch-long, slender dried mulberries that taste a million times better than their pale grub-like appearance might suggest, and pistachios that have been roasted with salt, saffron, and lemon that are impossible to stop eating. Somehow slightly less addictive, almonds toast up just as delicious this way, too.

Makes 2 cups

¼ teaspoon saffron threads, crushed to powder

Salt

2 cups raw pistachios or almonds

1 tablespoon cooking oil, olive or vegetable

½ lemon

Heat the oven to 350°F. If the saffron threads seem too soft to crush, dry them out for 15 minutes in a warm spot, like near the oven vent, and then crush them to powder with a mortar and pestle or in a small bowl with the back of a spoon. Combine the saffron, ½ teaspoon salt, and 2 tablespoons warm water in a medium mixing bowl and stir to dissolve. It takes a little while, but the salt will eventually melt. Add the nuts and the oil and stir for a good minute. Spread the mixture onto a baking sheet, put it in the oven, and set a timer for 10 minutes. Stir the nuts around with a spatula and roast until they are just getting tan inside, about 5 minutes. Tip them back into the mixing bowl, sprinkle them with ¼ teaspoon more salt, squeeze in the juice of the lemon half, and stir. Spread the nuts back on the sheet and bake another 5 minutes. When they are dry and lightly browned inside, they're done. The nuts will become crisp as they cool.

COLD-BRINED CARROTS

My friend Brooke and I shared an apartment after college, and I think she was a bit puzzled when I started showing real interest in cooking. We'd both worked in bars and restaurants, but instead of embracing hospitality, Brooke's thing was more, why go to all the trouble? Even when we'd throw a party and I'd start musing about a menu, what to make for appetizers, Brooke would shrug on her way to the liquor store, suggesting that I just cut up some vegetables, you know, for *coups d'état.* It's French, she'd tell me, for raw cut-up vegetables.

Brooke and I are still the best of friends, and today she's a great public-school teacher in Oakland. She doesn't teach French.

Makes 6 servings

2 tablespoons salt

2 tablespoons sugar

6 tablespoons red wine or cider vinegar

Ice

4 to 6 beautiful carrots, quartered or thinly sliced

In a mixing bowl, mix the salt, sugar, and vinegar with 2 cups cold water and whisk until completely dissolved. Add the ice and the carrots and refrigerate for at least an hour or up to 3 days.

* *Add 2 tablespoons whole toasted cumin, fennel, or coriander seeds.*
* *Add sliced jalapeños.*
* *Sliced cucumbers, fennel, radishes, and celery are also crunchy-fresh when brined.*

STUFFED CUCUMBER BARRELS

Crunchy and refreshing and tasting like solid little shots of white gazpacho, these barrels are light enough that you can eat a shipload and still be ready for dinner.

Makes 6 servings

3 tablespoons (about 20) toasted and finely chopped almonds (see page 9)

½ small garlic clove, pounded with a pinch of salt

2 tablespoons chopped parsley

1 teaspoon chopped marjoram

Pinch of cayenne or other ground hot pepper

1 tablespoon plus 1 teaspoon good olive oil

½ teaspoon grated lemon zest

Salt

1 or 2 slender cucumbers (about 12 ounces total), Painted Serpent, Persian, Armenian, or English

1 lemon (optional)

In a small bowl, combine the almonds, garlic paste, herbs, cayenne, oil, and lemon zest with a pinch of salt and mix well. Taste and adjust for salt and spiciness. Cut a slice from the cucumber and taste to see if it needs peeling (also, sometimes a rogue cucumber will be so bitter that it's unusable). I like to leave the skin on if it is not too tough, or at least to leave stripes of the skin for color. Cut the cucumber into ¾-inch chunks. With a melon baller or ¼ teaspoon measure, scoop out the center of each chunk, leaving enough to be the bottom of the barrel, so to speak. Lightly salt the barrels and squeeze on lemon juice if you like. Fill them with the almond mixture, mounding it up a little, arrange them on a platter, and pour the drinks.

* *Substitute mint, cilantro, or, sparingly, tarragon or dill for the marjoram.*

PIZZA DOUGH CRACKERS

Making good pizza dough takes hours, it's true, but the dough does most of the work. You just have to get it going and check on it every once in a while, like babies at nap time—soft, round, and needing to be tucked in as they rest.

Once risen and rolled, these crackers quickly bake up crispy and will keep, tightly covered, for many days. They are snacky-good just like that, and are platforms for everything from hummus to prosciutto to smoked fish. They're nice also with scrambled eggs or soft cheese, or slipped in under a salad. You can also, obviously, forgo crackers and make pizza. Equally obvious, perhaps, is that you can skip all the rising and rolling and make little toasts from the half a loaf you probably have on hand—just as good for spreading things on, but then, well . . . rising and rolling *can* be pretty fun.

Makes 6 servings

Sponge
1 teaspoon dry yeast
⅓ cup all-purpose flour
⅜ cup warm water

Dough
2 cups all-purpose flour

2 tablespoons rye flour (or whole wheat or other dark flour)

½ teaspoon salt

2 tablespoons olive oil, plus more for brushing

To make the sponge, mix the yeast, flour, and water in a bowl large enough to eventually hold all the ingredients (or in the bowl of a stand mixer). Using a whisk, stir well, then cover with a towel and let sit at room temperature until it has risen and become bubbly, about 30 minutes. You can leave the whisk in the bowl—you'll use it again. In another bowl, mix the flours and salt and set aside. When the sponge is ready, add not quite ¾ cup cold water and 1 cup of the flour mixture. Whisk well, cover, and let sit at room temperature until risen and bubbly again, about 30 minutes (now you're done with the whisk). With a wooden spoon, or paddle if using a mixer, mix in the remaining flour mixture and the oil. Stir till it's not so sticky, then use your hands to incorporate all the flour and knead into a smooth dough, either in the bowl or on a clean, flour-dusted counter.

Cover the dough in the bowl with a towel and let it rest at room temperature for 1 to 3 hours. Turn the puffy dough out onto the counter and knead again for a minute. Divide the dough into 8 equalish pieces and roll each of them under your palm until they are round and smooth. The motion is circular, like caressing a crystal ball and seeing crackers in your future. If the counter is too floury, the dough will just slide and won't grab and roll as it should. Set the balls on a tray and cover them with a towel to rest before rolling—right now they're too elastic. You can flatten them a little with your hand to speed things along, but give them at least 30 minutes to relax.

Heat the oven to 375°F. With a rolling pin on the floured counter, roll a dough ball very thin and about the size of a vinyl LP record. Using the tines of a fork, or a very cool thing called a docker, if you have one, perforate the dough all over—this prevents the crackers from puffing up and can be skipped if you want them, or some of them, very thin, fragile, and crispy. Transfer the round to a baking sheet and bake, checking frequently, until light brown and very crisp, about 10 minutes. Repeat with each of the balls. Once they're cooled, brushing the flour off the crackers and brushing on olive oil before breaking them into pieces gives them an appealing luster.

* *Immediately after brushing with oil, sprinkle the crackers with coarsely ground black pepper or toasted cumin or sesame seeds.*

CHARD WITH ALMONDS, RAISINS, AND PECORINO TO TOP PIZZA DOUGH CRACKERS

This recipe brings charm to often unloved chard and does likewise for kale, beet greens, and so on.

Makes 6 servings

1 big bunch chard

Salt

2 tablespoons cooking oil, olive or vegetable, or as needed

1 garlic clove, chopped

Crushed red pepper flakes

2 tablespoons toasted and chopped almonds (see page 9)

1 tablespoon raisins, plumped in hot water, drained, and chopped

Good olive oil

1 teaspoon red wine vinegar or sherry vinegar

Pecorino or Parmesan

Pizza dough crackers (page 21)

Tear or cut the leaves from the chard stems and wash them well, but do not spin them dry—it's good to have some water clinging to the leaves to help them steamily cook. Wash and thinly slice the stems. Bring ½ inch of water to a boil in a skillet, add ¼ teaspoon salt and the sliced stems and cook at a simmer until tender, about 15 minutes—but taste to be sure. Tip off the water, add the cooking oil, chard leaves, and a pinch more salt, and cook, stirring occasionally and adding splashes of water if the skillet gets dry before the chard is done. When tender, move the chard to the perimeter and add the garlic and red pepper flakes in the middle, with a bit more oil if it's dry. When the garlic smells good, about 1 minute, bring in the greens and mix well. Turn the chard onto a cutting board, squeezing out some of the liquid if it seems awash. Once cooled, chop it finely and stir it in a mixing bowl with the almonds, raisins, oil, vinegar, and a sensible grating of cheese. Taste, adjust, and spread, at room temperature or just warmed, on pizza dough crackers.

* *Stir in ¼ cup ricotta cheese for a creamier effect.*
* *Replace the raisins with sun-dried tomatoes.*

FISH TARTARE

On the West Coast there are great fish for eating raw, such as halibut and yellowtail jack, and back East, I like fluke. There are many more, I'm sure, and the number one criterion is that it be fresh, fresh, fresh—though not from freshwater; eating landlocked fish raw is perilous and not recommended. Many resources regarding which fish you ought and ought not to eat, raw or, for that matter, cooked, are at hand, starting with your trusted fishmonger. When you find a sparkling fillet of something you feel good about, make this light, bright tartare.

Makes 6 servings

6 ounces best fish fillet, well chilled

½ teaspoon salt

1 tablespoon chopped cilantro leaves and stems

1 scallion, all the white and most of the green parts, thinly sliced

1 tablespoon finely diced jalapeño (optional)

2 tablespoons good olive oil

Scant tablespoon lime juice

Pizza dough crackers (page 21) or other accompaniment

In a small mixing bowl, mix the fish with everything but the crackers. Taste, adjust, and serve right away on pieces of cracker or on thin crisp toasts, slices of cucumber, or sections of Belgian endive leaves.

* *Substitute basil, mint, tarragon, or dill for the cilantro and/or lemon for the lime.*
* *Quickly pickle some mustard seeds in a hot brine: In a small saucepan, combine 1 tablespoon mustard seeds with 1 teaspoon each salt, sugar, and red or white vinegar, and ¼ cup white wine or water; bring to a boil, turn off, and let cool. Make the tartare, but replace the cilantro with ½ teaspoon chopped tarragon, the jalapeños with ½ teaspoon Dijon mustard, and the lime with lemon; add some or all of the cooled and drained mustard seeds.*

FISH RILLETTES

This tasty recipe is from my colleague Jean-Pierre Moullé at Chez Panisse. JP is everything you imagine a French chef to be, a handsome hunter-forager-gardener who can whip up soufflés and gougères without a recipe before changing into, and completely pulling off, a pink polo shirt on his way to the tennis court. There were many lessons to learn, and I probably missed a lot, but I did manage to pick up this technique for turning a humble bit of fish into brilliant rillettes to spread on pizza dough crackers or little toasts.

Makes 6 servings

Lemon

1 small shallot, finely diced

Salt

4 tablespoons (½ stick) unsalted butter, softened at room temperature

2 to 3 ounces grilled, baked, or smoked fish, crumbled or chopped

2 tablespoons room-temperature plain yogurt or crème fraîche

Freshly ground black pepper

2 teaspoons finely chopped chives

2 teaspoons finely chopped chervil

1 teaspoon finely chopped tarragon

Grate the zest from about ¼ of the lemon and put it in a medium mixing bowl with the shallot, a pinch of salt, and juice from about half the lemon. Let sit for a few minutes to marinate the shallot, and then add everything else and mix well. Taste, adjust, and serve on something crisp with a glass of something cold and crisp.

FRICO

I have a friend who secretly likes Cheez Doodles. He knows he ought to say don'tle to the doodle because they're all fake and bright orange, and because he's the chef at a well-known restaurant famous for serving locally sourced, sustainably raised foods, and so my friend doesn't eat Cheez Doodles. No, never. Instead he turns to these crisp, cheesy, cracker-like frico. They are simple to make and, my friend swears, have the power to suppress baser urges.

Makes around 24 frico

1 cup finely grated Montasio or Piave cheese (see note)

¼ cup grated Parmesan

2 teaspoons cornmeal

2 teaspoons black sesame seeds (if you can't find them, substitute poppy seeds)

Heat the oven to 400°F. Mix all the ingredients together in a medium bowl and place tablespoonsful on a parchment-lined baking sheet, leaving room for the frico to spread as they bake. With your fingers, flatten the little piles to circles about 1½ inches in diameter and bake until lightly browned and fragrant, about 5 minutes. If they are baking unevenly, remove the ones that are done to a plate, rotate the baking sheet, and bake the rest a minute more. Set a timer or . . . burned cheese. The frico will be bendy while hot, but will crisp as they cool. Serve them right away with drinks, or cover them well. You can save them, unrefrigerated, for a day or two.

*   *If you can't find Montasio or Piave, use all Parmesan and half the cornmeal, or use another medium-aged cheese that you like. Pecorino or goat cheese can work, but if they're too soft, you may need to add a bit more cornmeal to hold the frico together. Bake just one at first and see.*

VEGETABLE FRITTERS

This Indian pakora-like batter has a bit of weight and flavor from chickpea flour, and a light but durable crunch from rice flour. It stays crisp and, as a bonus, is gluten-free if that's your thing.

Makes 6 servings

½ cup chickpea flour (available at some grocery stores and at Indian markets, where it's sometimes called besan or gram flour), plus more as needed

½ cup rice flour, plus more as needed

Baking soda

Salt

Bubbly water

Oil for frying

Raw vegetables, cut in fryable pieces (see ideas below)

In a medium bowl, combine the flours with pinches of baking soda and salt. Whisk in bubbly water until a thick batter forms—it should be a little thicker than cream. In a deep skillet or saucepan, heat the oil to 350°F. Dip a piece of vegetable in the batter and let the excess run off. If the batter is too thick, thin with more water; if too thin, add more of the flours. Start frying batches of vegetables when you've got the batter right, keeping the oil uncrowded. Drain the fritters on a rack or crumpled paper, sprinkle with salt, and serve.

* *To fry: asparagus, artichoke hearts, green beans, onion or sweet pepper rings, zucchini, peeled slices of winter squash or sweet potato, kale leaves, broccoli or cauliflower florets.*
* *Serve with cilantro-coconut chutney (page 255) or yogurt with pounded garlic and mint stirred in.*
* *Vegetable-frying oil can be strained and saved, refrigerated, for reuse for up to a week.*

FISH FRITTERS

It was years before I learned the kitchen skill of saying yes when asked if there was anything a guest could do to help. A friend of my son Milo reminded me recently of how potent that offer can be when she was over for dinner and wondered how she might help.

"You could eviscerate this bag of little smelt that I want to fry," I said, fishing, joking, and maybe kind of testing a bit.

She didn't miss a beat: "Which knife should I use?"

A keeper, and Milo knew it, too, blushing a little and bending to special sauce-making for cover. She finished all the smelts neatly and we dredged and fried them and ate them hot off crumpled newspaper, licking our fingers to sooth the burn—and for that tasty/trashy sauce—but also conspiratorially, in solidarity, the shared task bridging our differences. It's what accepting help from someone can do, how cooking (especially frying!) can level and unite. Barn raisings and quilting bees had the same power, one imagines, but they are nearly extinct. Cooking survives.

I love a little fried something to snack on while standing around chatting, often right in the kitchen. There's usually a bottle of white wine open at this point, and stirring a little of it into flour makes a crisp, almost lacy batter for any kind of fish—little strips of mild groundfish like sole, pollock, hake, lingcod, halibut, or flounder are especially nice. Serve with a dab of aïoli (page 265) or spoonfuls of either caponatina (page 257) or fresh turmeric salsa (page 263).

Oil for frying

10 ounces fish, cut into strips

Salt

½ cup all-purpose flour, plus more as needed

1 cup white wine, plus more as needed

In a deep skillet or saucepan, heat 3 or 4 inches of fry oil to 350°F. Sprinkle the fish lightly with salt.

Meanwhile, combine the flour and ¼ teaspoon salt in a medium bowl. Whisk in the wine until a thick batter forms—it should be a little thicker than cream. Dip a piece of fish in the batter and let the excess run off. If the batter is too thick, thin it with more wine; if too thin, add more flour. Start frying batches of fish when you've got the batter right, keeping the oil uncrowded. Drain on a rack or crumpled paper, sprinkle with salt, and serve.

* *Fish-frying oil cannot really be reused and should be discarded.*

TO START: FIRST COURSES

I don't think I ever really had a meal that included a first course until I moved to Italy, where everybody eats that way, even at lunch. The *primo piatto* I remember best was made by the mother of a friend on the evening of a trying day. I was eager to find some work, knowing that the money we'd saved wouldn't last long, and had been out on the job hunt. I had experience as a waiter, and though my Italian was very bad, I knew a few phrases and had memorized a particularly important one to use while applying at the restaurant that a friend of a friend sent me to. His name was Pino, and he had some connection to the place, so I went in, found the manager, and said what I had committed to memory: "Pino sent me. He said that maybe I can work here." Sounded better, more convincing, I thought, in my ridiculous Italian.

Only as I was reciting my bit did it occur to me that I might just need a follow-up phrase, that an American waiter who could tell customers only that he'd been sent by Pino would at best be useless, and might actually be creepy, like I was going to whack one of them. The manager must have thought something similar, but he was nice, if puzzled, and paused before replying with several sentences of which I understood only the word *Pino*. It was now my turn to pause, cursing myself for somehow failing to fore-see the futility of this, and searching my tiny vocabulary for a response. What I came up with, really my only other phrase, was fairly inappropri-ate to the situation, and I am grateful to the manager for not hooting in my face.

"*Mi piace pancetta*," I said, a little loudly, which basically means, "I like bacon!"

He looked at me, his suspicions that Americans were pork-fattened fools confirmed. "*Oh, si?*"

"*Si*," I said, less loudly but no less stupidly. "*Si, mi piace pancetta.*" I nod-ded solemnly as if this cleared things up, as if my love of cured pork belly was all the qualification one needed for employment.

He smiled kindly, bless him, and said, "*Anch'io.*" Me, too.

That night, at my friend's mother's house, still jobless, I told the story, endured the laughter, and, after a glass of prosecco, joined in with it. I was grateful to be at Mamma's house, and my failure faded further as she brought the first course to the table: tiny eels, each the size of half a length of spaghetti, served with the oil they were cooked in. They were so very good, and so was the garlicky oil we sopped up with bread until our chins shone with it. I had never had something so deliciously simple and perfect. When I asked my friend's mom what they were called, and she paused, I was reminded of my humiliation at the restaurant and won-dered if I had made another blunder. But it was she who was embarrassed—eels like this were a forbidden delicacy, caught and

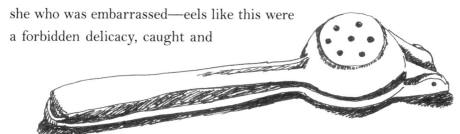

brought, perhaps, from somewhere they ought not to be.

"*Contrabbando,*" she said.

I didn't really understand, but when she said nothing more, declared, "*Mi piace contrabbando!*" pleased that my vocabulary had grown, if esoterically, and sensing that things might still work out—I'd learn Italian, find a job, drink more prosecco, and eat more pancetta and baby eels (which, by the way, are not illegal, just very expensive).

And I did.

A great first course announces your intention to put on the kind of dinner that will leave no one feeling uninterested, ignored, or disengaged. Color plays a big part in this, visual appeal as a social rallying point, something we all appreciate and so, in a way, unites us. Also, a little *ta-da* can dissolve any moments of awkwardness that sometimes come at the beginning of an evening's gathering. We've all felt it. Maybe the hors d'oeuvres weren't strong enough to break the ice. Or they did, and it somehow refroze, but once everyone is seated, watered, wined, and starting in on beautiful platters, the heat will come back on and take off any chill. I try to make starting dishes eye-catching enough to create a little ripple, but not a riptide—to feed and gather, not shock and scatter. Done right, the first course settles us in at the table.

Spring

AGNOLOTTI DEL PLIN IN BRODO WITH SWEET PEAS

When I had these little stuffed pastas at a hillside restaurant in Barolo, Italy, they were served not bobbing in brodo, but cozy and dry, tucked into a folded white napkin. No sauce, just delicious meaty dimpled pillows to uncover and devour. I learned later that there was in fact broth involved: the agnolotti had been boiled in it, which explained the almost supernatural flavor that they delivered. In turn, the broth became slightly thickened by the pasta starch, and could then be used to make, say, a second-course chicken *fricassea*, as happened at my happy hillside lunch in Barolo. Genius.

I fly respectfully in the face of tradition, happily stuffing agnolotti with a variety of fillings—ricotta, greens, mushrooms, and so on—while admitting, enthusiastically, that the finely textured mixture of braised meats and greens that typically fills agnolotti deserves its good reputation and, further, can use up the scraps of last night's feast in a tasty and elegant way. Almost any braise will work, mixed with well-cooked greens and a grating of cheese. As is so often the case, a measure of pork—braised belly or shoulder, pancetta, prosciutto, or mortadella—is advised.

Makes 6 servings

1 tablespoon cooking oil, olive or vegetable

2 ounces pancetta, sliced bacon-thick, then cut crosswise into sticks

3 ounces spinach leaves, or chard leaves, stems removed, washed and drained, but not spun dry

Salt

8 ounces leftover braised short ribs (page 189) or duck leg (page 172) or other braised meat or poultry (about 1 cup)

⅓ cup grated pecorino or Parmesan

2 tablespoons unsalted butter, at soft room temperature

½ teaspoon red wine vinegar or sherry vinegar (optional)

1 batch egg pasta dough (page 146)

1¼ pounds fresh peas, shelled

3 cups brodo (page 42)

Heat a large skillet to medium. Add the oil and the pancetta and cook until it turns translucent and just starts to brown around the edges, less than 5 minutes. Remove the pancetta with a slotted spoon and set it aside. If you feel as if there's too much fat in the pan (there probably isn't), take a little out, and then add the greens and a pinch of salt.

Cook until the greens are very tender, stirring occasionally and adding water when needed to keep them moist. Set the greens aside on a tilted plate to let any liquid run out as they cool.

Combine the braised meat, pancetta, and drained greens and put them through the fine holes of a meat grinder. They can also be pulsed in a food processor or chopped by hand—the mixture should be very fine, but not pureed entirely smooth. Mix in the cheese and butter, taste, and correct. Sometimes, if the meats were braised with little or no wine, a bit of red wine vinegar or sherry vinegar is nice to cut through the fat.

Start rolling out the pasta, making it incrementally thinner until it is just translucent, about the thickness of heavy paper or cardstock. On my machine, this is number 6. Because pasta dough doesn't always behave the same way, I sometimes roll the dough through 6 twice, if I want it thinner, but not so thin as number 7.

On a floured surface, cut the sheet of pasta into lengths of about 16 inches. Keep one to work with first, sprinkle the rest with flour, stack them, and set them aside, covered so that they don't dry out. Brush any loose flour off the sheet you're starting with and cut it in half lengthwise so that you have 2 long strips about 3 inches wide. Lightly brush or spritz the strips of pasta with water so they will seal when folded.

Laying a strip in front of you like a keyboard and using a pastry bag or small spoon, place teaspoonfuls of the filling along the center of the strips in rows, leaving a good inch between each dollop. Fold the pasta away from you and over the filling. Starting at one end so that the air can escape from the other end, smooth the dough around the lumps of filling. Your fingers should slide over the pasta as you go—if the pasta is grabbing and wrinkling, dip your fingers in flour before you curve them around each bump of filling. Repeat with the other pasta strip. When both strips are sealed, trim the long side where the edges meet to tidy it up using a sharp knife, pizza wheel, or—prettiest—a zigzag pasta cutter.

If you were to now simply cut in between the bumps, you'd have little ravioli. Very cute, but cuter still if you can manage the agnolotti roll-and-cut: Lift the near edge of the strip a little, as if you're peeking under the rug, but halfheartedly. Folding it partly away from you, but not quite in half, cut through the fold to make individual agnolotti, which should look like pregnant little envelopes that are almost coming open. Work your way down the strip, cutting and tossing the finished agnolotti with flour and coating them well to keep them from sticking to each other. Spread them onto a floured tray. Repeat with the rest of the pasta and filling; refrigerate the agnolotti, uncovered, until you're ready to boil them. If you're not cooking them the same day, freeze them on the tray, and then bag them and keep them frozen until you're ready to cook (do not defrost before boiling).

Bring a big pot of water to a boil and add salt. Drop one agnolotti and a few peas into the water. Taste them both after a few minutes to figure out your timing—do they cook at the same rate, or do you need to start one before the other? In a saucepan, bring the brodo to a simmer while you formulate a plan. Drop the agnolotti and peas into the boiling water and drain when done. Divide the pasta and peas into warm soup bowls and ladle the brodo over them. Eat hot.

BRODO

Making brodo is just like making stock, except that instead of pouring water over raw bones, you roast the bones first and pour previously made stock over them. The result is richly flavored double stock.

Making the effort to simmer up just a tiny batch of brodo makes no sense, so this recipe yields plenty more than you'll need for six bowls of agnolotti. Save the rest for the next dinner, and because having servings of restorative brodo in your freezer is like a savory first-aid kit for when someone gets a cold.

Makes about 3 quarts

Cooking oil, olive or vegetable

2 pounds chicken, turkey, or duck bones (necks, backs, wings, and so on)

1 yellow onion, thinly sliced

3 thyme sprigs

3 parsley sprigs

1 bay leaf

6 black peppercorns

½ cup white wine or ¼ cup sherry

3 quarts chicken stock (page 44)

Salt

Heat the oven to 450°F.

Sprinkle a rimmed baking sheet with a little oil, rub it around, spread the bones on the sheet, and roast them until browned, about 30 minutes.

Meanwhile, heat a soup pot to high and add 3 tablespoons oil and then the onion. Stir until the onion gets going, then turn the heat to medium and cook, stirring occasionally, until it is lightly browned. Lower the heat a little and keep cooking to caramelize the onion—it will add nice color and a little savory sweetness to the brodo. When the onion is quite brown, sizzling a little, but not smelling burned, turn off the heat, cover, and let sit to deglaze itself for 5 minutes. Stir with a wooden spoon, scraping up the brown glaze from the bottom. Turn the heat back on to medium and brown the onion some more, again stopping when it sizzles and the bottom of the pot is glazed. Cover, wait, and scrape

again, then add the thyme, parsley, bay leaf, and peppercorns. Stir for a minute, add the wine, raise the heat to high, and continue to stir while it bubbles for a minute more. Add the roasted bones and deglaze the baking sheet with a ladle of stock, scraping with a wooden spoon to dislodge any flavorful bits, then add the deglazings and the remaining stock. Bring to a boil, then immediately lower the heat to a simmer and skim off any fat and foam that has risen. Keep the brodo just at a bubble, so it doesn't reduce too much, for 2 hours. Strain, stir in ½ teaspoon salt, taste, and adjust.

CHICKEN STOCK

Makes about 6 quarts

3 pounds chicken bones

1 large yellow onion, halved and
peeled

1 large carrot, peeled and chopped
into a few chunks

2 celery stalks, chopped into a few
chunks

4 parsley sprigs

4 thyme sprigs

1 bay leaf

In a large stockpot, cover all the ingredients with cold water by 4 or 5 inches
and bring to a boil over high heat. Immediately turn the heat down and skim
off the foam that rises to the surface. Cook at a low simmer for 3 hours, then
strain. Let the stock sit for 5 minutes, then skim off the fat with a ladle. If you
aren't cooking with the stock right away, refrigerate it, uncovered, until cold.
Freeze the chicken stock in quart or pint containers, and it will come in so
handy later.

ASPARAGUS AND FISH CONFIT SALAD WITH GOLDEN BEETS, FENNEL, AND AÏOLI

Cooking fish slowly in olive oil reveals luscious depths of flavor and texture that can't be found elsewhere short of salt-curing or smoking. A few flakes of this rich fish on a plate of simply cooked spring vegetables, served with a bowl of aïoli made with new garlic, can be a lunch or a first course that conjures hope—faith that soon the summer will come, and with it, tomatoes and sweet peppers that can easily replace golds and pale greens with ripe reds.

Makes 6 servings

1 bunch golf-ball-size golden beets

Salt

1 teaspoon red wine vinegar

Good olive oil

1 pound fish fillets, ideally ½ inch thick—something not too delicate (I like various types of amberjacks, also halibut, sea bass . . .)

Freshly ground black pepper

Crushed red pepper flakes

2 teaspoons fennel seeds, toasted and coarsely ground (see page 9)

1 fennel bulb, trimmed and cut lengthwise into ½-inch-thick wedges

1¼ pounds asparagus, tough ends snapped off and (unless very thin) lower ⅔ of stalks peeled

Lemon

1 cup aïoli (page 265)

Leaves to garnish (see note)

Heat the oven to 425°F.

Cut the greens off the beets and save them, if they're in good shape, for another use (page 23). Rinse the beets thoroughly and boil them in well-salted water or, even better, roast them (see the instructions on page 62). Using your hands, slip the skins off the cooled beets and cut the beets into slices or wedges. Dress them with the red wine vinegar, a tablespoon of oil, and ¼ teaspoon salt. Taste, adjust, and set aside.

Meanwhile, season the fish with ½ teaspoon salt, black pepper, red pepper flakes, and the fennel seeds. While you let the salt soak in for a few minutes, find a skillet or baking dish that will accommodate the fish in a single layer with very little extra space. Add enough oil to cover the bottom of the skillet or dish, fit the fish in, and then add more oil to just cover. Put the skillet over a low flame, or the baking dish in a 250°F oven (after the beets are out and cooling), and cook—turning the pieces over when the bottom half is looking done—until the fish has mostly turned opaque, but still has a few little translucent spots. Transfer the fish and oil to a shallow bowl or dish, and set it aside to cool.

Bring a pot of water to a boil for cooking the fennel and the asparagus. Add salt, and once it boils, taste the water and add more salt if needed so that it tastes not like seawater but on its way there—brackish. Boil the fennel until tender, about 5 minutes, and then dip it out and spread the wedges on a plate to cool. Repeat with the asparagus.

When you're ready to assemble the salad, put the fennel and asparagus in a mixing bowl and dress with a tablespoon of oil, a squeeze of lemon, and a sprinkle of salt. When they taste right, arrange them, the beets, and the fish on a serving platter. Drizzle with a little of the fish-cooking oil and juices. Either pass the bowl of aïoli or dollop it around on the platter. You can also thin it with a little water and spoon it over the vegetables and fish in stripes or spirals. Garnish the platter with sprigs of herbs, rocket, or cress.

* *Note: Every composed salad says "garden" more clearly with a little tuft or scattering of tender salad leaves or herbs such as watercress or other cress, wild rocket, baby red mustard greens, basil, mint, or chervil. They can be lightly dressed or, if very small and fragile, left undressed.*
* *As the season changes, replace the asparagus with green beans . . . add wedges of tomatoes, strips of roasted peppers (page 85), boiled new potatoes, and so on.*

FRIED WILD SHRIMP WITH FRESH TURMERIC, SESAME, AND SNAP PEA SALAD

There are many delicious ways that I like to eat shrimp, and for every one there is a very good reason why I never buy farm-raised shrimp. The conditions in which they are raised are an unappetizing horror of a story, so I won't tell it here, but you don't have to dive deep to find out all that's wrong about farmed shrimp, and I urge you to do so. The good news is that wild shrimp, caught the no-turtles-hurt, minimal-bycatch way that you and I would net them were we shrimpers, are available. If your fishmonger doesn't want to answer questions, I suggest finding a new one who does. We humans are not the only ones who like to eat sweet shrimp, so I try to leave lots in the sea and fry just a few for dinner.

Makes 6 servings

Salt

½ pound snap peas, stems and strings removed, bias-cut into thirds

Oil for frying

1 cup all-purpose flour

1½ teaspoons ground turmeric

3 teaspoons sesame seeds, all white or with a quarter black

1 cup white wine

4 or 5 radishes, thinly sliced

3 scallions, all the white part and most of the green, thinly sliced

Fresh turmeric salsa (page 263)

Good olive oil

18 medium-size wild-caught shrimp, peeled, tails left on, deveined

Bring a pot of well-salted water to a boil and add the snap peas. Cook until still quite crunchy, about 1½ minutes, and then dip them out and spread them on a plate to cool.

Heat a pot with 4 inches of frying oil. You'll know it's ready to fry when it reaches 350°F or when a drop of the batter (which you're about to make) sizzles spiritedly, but not frighteningly, nor does it sink silently to the bottom. Also, heat the oven to warm (about 200°F) and set up a rack or crumpled paper on a tray or plate for the fried shrimp to drain on.

Make the batter by mixing the flour, turmeric, 2 teaspoons of the sesame seeds, and ¼ teaspoon salt in a bowl and whisking in the wine.

In a mixing bowl, dress the cooled snap peas, radishes, and scallions with a pinch of salt, 2 tablespoons of the turmeric salsa, and some olive oil. Mix well and put the salad on a platter that the shrimp will fit on, too— now you're ready to start frying.

Sprinkle ½ teaspoon salt on the shrimp, put them in the batter, and turn them over until completely coated. Quickly and carefully, with both hands, start lifting shrimp from the batter and easing them into the fry pot. There may be too many to fry at a go, which is why the oven is warm. Turn the shrimp if they're not submerged in oil, and when they are golden brown and cooked through, about 4 minutes, dip them out to drain on the rack or crumpled paper, sprinkle them lightly with salt, then keep them warm in the oven while you swiftly fry the rest. Arrange the fried shrimp on the platter with the salad, spoon the rest of the salsa around, and sprinkle with the remaining sesame seeds.

*   *Make a healthy little tea by steeping the turmeric and ginger peelings with a few mint sprigs. Sip thoughtfully.*
*   *Shrimp-frying oil cannot really be reused and should be discarded.*

GRILLED ASPARAGUS WITH HOMEMADE PANCETTA AND HAZELNUT SALSA

Some farmers sell what is called field-run produce, gorgeous stuff that comes straight from the field, but is unsorted, so you'll get, say, asparagus ranging in thickness from drinking-straw-size to thumb-size. Randomness can be inspirational, compelling a cook to focus on each stalk, figure how it should be cooked, and intuit when it's done. That said, it is a real pleasure to open a box of asparagus that has been sorted for the fattest, most succulent spears, the kind that need only simple boiling or can even be shaved to eat raw.

For grilling, I like it all, fat and skinny. The fat ones are best peeled and boiled in salted water before hitting the grill, but the skinniest ones can, once the tough ends are snapped off, go straight on, oiled and salted, and, when cooked through, will have a pleasing, but not choking, char.

Makes 6 servings

1 shallot, finely diced

2 teaspoons red wine vinegar, or
1 teaspoon red wine vinegar and
1 teaspoon sherry vinegar

Freshly ground black pepper

Salt

Cooking oil, olive or vegetable

2 or 3 thick slices pancetta (about
6 ounces; page 53), cut across into
little strips

2 tablespoons chopped parsley

1 garlic clove and 3 or 4 sage
leaves, pounded with a pinch of salt

¼ cup hazelnuts, toasted and
chopped (see page 9)

Good olive oil

1¼ pounds asparagus, tough ends
snapped off and, if fat, lower ⅔ of
stalks peeled, boiled in salted water
until tender

Lemon

Leaves to garnish (see note,
page 46)

Prepare a hot grill (see page 10).

To make the salsa, combine the shallot, vinegar, pepper, and ¼ teaspoon salt and let marinate

for 5 minutes. Meanwhile, heat a small skillet to medium and add ½ tablespoon cooking oil and the pancetta. Cook, stirring occasionally, until the pancetta is transparent and browning on the edges, or until crispy, if you prefer. Drain and set the pancetta aside. In a small bowl, mix the parsley, garlic and sage paste, hazelnuts, pancetta, marinated shallots, ¼ teaspoon salt, and 3 tablespoons olive oil. Stir, taste, adjust, and set aside while you grill the asparagus.

Coat the asparagus with cooking oil and season with salt. When the fire is ready and the grates are hot and clean, grill the asparagus until it is nicely colored and tender. Remove it from the grill, dress it with a squeeze of lemon and splash of olive oil, and arrange it on a warm platter. Spoon half of the salsa over the asparagus and pass the rest at the table.

* *If you are not up to grilling, roast the asparagus in a 450°F oven instead.*

PANCETTA

Curing pork belly for pancetta is simple and satisfying. True, pink curing salt must be found (at your butcher or online) and a way to hang the pancetta in your fridge rigged up (string and paper clips are what I use), but other than that, it really just takes time.

The amounts given here are for curing 3 pounds of belly, but you could cure any amount (though maybe not too small a piece—at least 1½ pounds) using this ratio: the salt amount is 3 percent of the belly by weight; sugar is 0.33 percent. For the pink curing salt, I use half the amount recommended on the package.

Makes 2 nice paperback-book-size slabs

2 tablespoons plus 2 teaspoons salt

¼ teaspoon pink curing salt

1 teaspoon sugar

3 pounds skin-on pork belly, split into 2 squares

1 tablespoon fennel seeds

2 teaspoons coriander seeds

4 juniper berries

4 bay leaves, crumbled

Freshly ground black pepper

Crushed red pepper flakes

1 tablespoon finely chopped rosemary leaves

¼ teaspoon ground cinnamon

Combine both salts and the sugar and coat the pork belly with the mixture, patting it on to make it stick. Place the pancetta-to-be in a shallow dish, sprinkle any extra salt mixture on top, cover, and refrigerate for 12 days, turning the belly over every 2 days. The liquid drawn from the meat by the salt may collect in the dish and does not need to be drained off.

After 12 days, it's time to coat the pancetta with the spices and herbs and begin the drying process. Heat a small skillet to medium and add the fennel and coriander seeds. Toast the spices, shaking the skillet occasionally, until they start to hop around a little and smell good, about 30 seconds. Tip them into a clean spice mill or mortar, add the juniper and bay, and grind medium fine. In a small bowl, combine the ground spices with the black and red pepper, rosemary, and cinnamon. Pat the belly pieces dry and coat them with the spices and herbs. Using a skewer or thin-bladed knife, make a hole in a corner of each of the belly pieces and push a string through it for hanging. Hang the pancetta in the back of your refrigerator, where the temperature is more stable, for 3 weeks. (I hang them from the rod supporting the shelf in my fridge. It looks pretty authentic and Old World, dangling there in the back of the fridge as if in a curing cave, but if that doesn't work for you, pancetta can also be cured on a wire rack with the skin side down.)

At that point, you can scrape off the spices and herbs and cut slices as needed, trimming the hard skin off only the part you are cooking with—leave the rest on there to protect the meat from overdrying. Depending on how quickly you use the pancetta, you can just leave it hanging. It does get pretty hard after about 2 months, so if you won't use it all up by then, either freeze half, tightly wrapped, or give it away to a lucky, pork-appreciative friend.

SAVORY FLAKY TART WITH ONIONS, OLIVES, AND ANCHOVIES

Long-cooked onions, anchovies, and olives baked on dough is a common dish, especially in southern France, and goes by a name I will not say—it's the sort of dish that provokes strong feelings of loyalty to tradition and claims or denials of authenticity. There are those who make it one way, those who make it another, and calling my version by name would only put me in the crosshairs *culinaires.* Call it what you will and have another slice.

Makes 8 to 10 servings

¼ cup cooking oil, olive or vegetable

2 large yellow onions, thinly sliced lengthwise

1 teaspoon salt

1 tablespoon chopped thyme or 1 teaspoon chopped marjoram, or both

1 chilled, unbaked round of flaky tart dough (recipe follows)

Scant tablespoon all-purpose flour

12 to 20 anchovy fillets, sliced in half lengthwise

¾ cup Niçoise olives, pitted and torn in half

1 egg, beaten

Heat the oven to 425°F.

Heat a large skillet over high heat and add the cooking oil, then the onions and salt. Stir until it gets going, then turn to medium and cook, stirring occasionally, until soft and very lightly browned, 15 to 20 minutes. Use a lid or a splash of water if the onions color too much before getting soft.

Taste a piece after 10 minutes or so and add more salt if needed. Add the herbs and continue cooking until completely soft; if, when you bite a piece, you hear crunching, keep going. Don't lose your nerve, and they will be done in 20 to 30 minutes. A little coloring is okay, but it's better to keep it fresh-tasting and not caramel sweet. When they're done, tip the onions into a colander set over a bowl to drain for 5 minutes. Reserve any liquid.

Set the tart round on a baking sheet lined with parchment paper (a round, flat baking pan, like for pizza, works really well here) and sprinkle the flour over it to cover all but the outer inch of dough. Spoon the onions in an even layer over the floured part and arrange the anchovy fillets and olive pieces on top of the onions in a pattern of your choosing. I suggest argyle or a nice houndstooth. Turn the exposed edge of the dough up over the filling, pleating it with little folds as you go around. If the dough is still cold and too firm to bend, leave it a few minutes to soften so that it doesn't crack. Brush the crust with egg so it will shine.

Bake until well browned, about 45 minutes. With a spatula, carefully lift the edge of the tart and peek at the bottom side—it should be very well colored. If not, bake for 5 minutes more. Let the tart cool—preferably off the pan and paper and sitting on a wire rack—for a few minutes while you warm up a little of the reserved onion cooking liquid. Slice the tart into wedges and spoon the warm liquid over it on the plates.

* *A salad of lettuces and soft herbs, or really any green or vegetable salad, and glasses of cold rosé are perfect alongside.*

Flaky Tart Dough

Like most doughs, this one contains very few ingredients, but that doesn't mean it's simple to make. Good dough-making, especially a buttery, tender one like this, takes a practiced hand. If you are lucky enough to be friends with an experienced pie or tart maker, go to them with gifts, offers, and kind words and ask for help. If not, these tarts are worth buying a bag of flour and a pound of butter for and starting to develop that sure, light touch. Maybe—probably— you're a natural. I always make a two-tart batch—one for a savory tart for tonight's first course, and the other one to roll out and freeze for a fruit tart (pages 276, 291, 299, and 314) another night.

1¾ cups all-purpose flour

¼ cup whole wheat flour

¼ teaspoon salt

1½ sticks cool unsalted butter

½ cup or less ice water

Sift the flours and salt together. The butter should be cool, not refrigerator-hard, but not soft like for creaming for cookies. The trick of this dough is mixing the butter quickly and thoroughly with the flour so that it becomes the consistency of fresh bread crumbs. If the butter starts too soft, or gets too soft from overhandling, you'll lose the flaky tenderness you want. Start by cutting the butter lengthwise into thin slabs and tossing them in the bowl of flour so that they get coated and don't stick together. Shake the flour off the butter slabs and cut them into sticks. Flour them again, shake off the excess, cut the sticks into little squares and put them back in the bowl of flour. With your fingertips, start crushing the butter squares, as if you're making the gesture for lucre, or trying to get its stain off your fingers. Don't use your whole hot hand, fingers only. When it looks crumbly like fresh bread crumbs and you see only small smears of butter, no chunks big enough to melt and create holes in what will be a thinly rolled crust, begin adding the cold water. Keep moving quickly, mixing in just enough so that when you squeeze a handful of dough, it seriously considers staying together, but doesn't quite. Stop adding water before the dough gets at all wet: it should be dry in spots and fall-apart-y. It will manage to pull itself together as it rests and chills, as I often hope to.

Gather half of the dough into a ball, wrap it in plastic, and flatten it into a disc about 4½ inches across and 1 inch thick. Repeat with the remaining dough and refrigerate the 2 discs for at least a couple of hours and up to overnight. You can freeze one of them or, if your freezer space allows, you can roll it out before freezing for more convenient use later.

Place a chilled disc of dough on a well-floured sturdy surface, sprinkle some flour on top, and press the dough down all around with a rolling pin. Sprinkle a little more flour if needed and begin rolling from the middle in all directions. If it feels too hard, leave it to warm up for 10 minutes. Cracking around the edges is inevitable, but use your hands to press back together any major faults that form. Keep rolling and flouring as needed until the dough is thin and about 13 inches across. Slide it onto the baking pan and pop it in the freezer for 5 minutes to firm up while you sweep up.

* *Okay, there is another way to make buttery pastry dough that I learned from my friend Clover. I use it mainly for making sweet tarts like the ones on pages 287 and 317, and sometimes for flaky dough. It's easier, and the result is only a tiny bit tougher in an almost unnoticeable way. Start by freezing the stick of butter for an hour. Grate it through the big holes of a box grater into the flour/sugar/salt mixture. Stir with your fingers until all the bits are separated, then set aside for 10 to 15 minutes, depending on your room's temperature, to let the butter defrost. Proceed with the technique above from when you start crushing the butter squares.*
* *Yet another of the many uses for this flaky dough occurred to me when my son Liam requested chicken pot pie for his eleventh birthday dinner. When I hear "chicken pot pie," I always think of the frozen kind—the ones that I inevitably forked into too soon, steam-burning my mouth as a hungry teen—but I wanted a big pie, enough for a dozen, and doubted that I had the skills to avoid the dreaded soggy bottom. The answer: avoid the bottom crust altogether. I rolled out an oval of trusty flaky dough and laid it atop chicken and vegetable stew lightly thickened with flour and butter. Brushed up with egg and baked brown, this pastry is so buttery-crisp that no one will care, or even notice, how many crusts there are.*

SWEET PEA RISOTTO

Two things about sweet pea risotto: Always cook and puree some of the peas to stir in for extra green goodness (works for asparagus risotto, too). The other thing is one of many chestnuts learned from my longtime colleague, the much-admired cook and writer David Tanis: always say "sweet peas" instead of just "peas." Sounds better. David, who also literally wrote the book on corn, would go on to describe how to make this risotto: "First, you take a pea . . ." Leek soup? "First, you take a . . ."

Makes 6 servings

1½ pounds English peas, shelled (about 1½ cup)

8 tablespoons (1 stick) butter

Salt

1 tablespoon olive oil

1 yellow onion, diced

2 cups short-grained Italian rice, such as Arborio or Carnaroli (I have also made good risotto with short-grained Japanese rice)

¾ cup dry white wine

6 cups chicken stock (page 44), hot

1 cup grated Parmesan

2 tablespoons thinly sliced mint leaves (from 2 to 3 sprigs)

In a smallish saucepan, combine ¾ cup of the peas with 2 tablespoons of the butter, ¼ teaspoon salt, and water to nearly cover—the top tier of peas should be above the waterline. Bring to a boil, lower to a simmer, and cook until very tender—cooking time will depend on the nature and age of your peas: less for little sugary tykes, more for the starchy grown-ups. Don't undercook the grown-ups. Do note how long the peas take to cook, as this will determine when you add the rest of them to the risotto later. Add water as needed to keep the peas stewy, but not too, and when they're done, push them through a sieve, pass them through a food mill, or spin them in a blender or food processor. Set the puree aside while you make the risotto.

Heat a 10- to 12-inch skillet over high heat and add the oil and 2 tablespoons of the butter, then the onion and ¼ teaspoon salt. Stir until the mixture sizzles noisily, then reduce the heat to medium and cook, stirring occasionally, until soft, 15 to 20 minutes. Use a lid and/or a splash of water if the onion colors too much before getting soft. Raise the heat to medium-high, add the rice and 1 teaspoon salt, and cook for 2 minutes to toast the rice a little, stirring frequently. Add the wine, let it bubble for 30 seconds, and then lower  the heat to medium and add 1 cup of the hot chicken stock. Keep the skillet at a lively but not ferocious simmer and stir to keep the rice from sticking. When the liquid is nearly gone, add another cup of stock. Repeat the additions of stock, stirring frequently, and add the reserved uncooked peas at the appropriate moment: it takes about 20 minutes from the time the wine went in for the risotto to be done, so if the peas for the puree took, say, 5 minutes, add the whole peas when there's 5 to go. Keep simmering and adding stock (or water if you've run out) until the rice is tender but still has a little bite.

Add the remaining 4 tablespoons butter, the pureed peas, and the Parmesan and stir energetically for 15 seconds. Taste, adjust, and let the risotto rest, off the heat and covered, to gather itself for a couple of minutes. Sprinkle it with mint and serve.

* *Substitute a bunch of asparagus for the peas, stewing and pureeing some of the tender stalks and adding the tips, halved or quartered as needed, to the risotto near the end.*

WILD SALMON GRAVLAX
WITH SHAVED ASPARAGUS SALAD

When I first started at Chez Panisse, Peggy Smith and Gilbert Pilgram were in charge of the Café kitchen. They were both wonderful chefs who have gone on to great things, and I still think about, and am inspired by, their delicious menus. Gilbert and Peggy did magic with humble ingredients like carrots and cabbage, and even more with luxuries like truffles and foie gras. One dish that I no longer make, but remember with delight, was a salt-cured whole foie gras that we'd cut in chunks and freeze and then shave very thinly over herb and rocket salads or, in spring, ribbons of raw asparagus.

Though I think foie gras is one of the tiniest parts of a huge problem in the way so much of our livestock is raised, and I do love its buttery duckiness, I don't cook with it anymore—and it's actually illegal here in California! Asparagus, on the other stalk, no one gets upset about, so I cook it all kinds of ways, or not at all, as in this salad for when there are fat spears of it to shave and dress and eat with just-as-luxurious wild salmon gravlax.

Makes 6 servings

1 bunch beets, golden, Chioggia, or red

Salt

2 teaspoons red wine vinegar

Good olive oil

1 shallot, finely diced

1 teaspoon white wine vinegar

1 teaspoon lemon juice

Freshly ground black pepper

8 to 12 thick asparagus stalks, tough ends snapped off

Handful (about 3 medium carrots' worth) cold-brined carrots (page 17)

2 tablespoons roughly chopped chervil or mint or both

12 or more slices wild salmon gravlax (recipe follows)

3 tablespoons crème fraîche (page 248) or yogurt, thinned with a little water or milk so that it will flow, but slowly, from a spoon

Leaves to garnish (see note, page 46)

Heat the oven to 425°F.

Cut the greens off the beets and save them, if they're in good shape, for another use (page 23). Rinse the beets well and put them in a small baking pan with ½ inch of water and a generous sprinkling of salt. Cover the pan with foil and roast until a paring knife meets very little resistance when slipped into the center of a beet—check at 45 minutes. If they are firm at all, add more water if needed and keep cooking. If you don't want to light the oven just for beets, you can also boil/simmer them in plenty of salted water. Take them out when tender and let cool. Using your hands, slip the skins off and cut the beets into slices or wedges, then dress with the red wine vinegar, 1 tablespoon oil, and ¼ teaspoon salt. Taste, adjust, and set aside.

Meanwhile, in a small bowl, mix the shallot with ¼ teaspoon salt, the white wine vinegar, lemon juice, and ground black pepper; let the mixture marinate a few minutes for the vinaigrette. Stir in 3 tablespoons oil.

Shave the stalks of asparagus lengthwise into ribbons. I do this using a fork to stab and steady the stalk at the thick end, and a Y-shaped vegetable peeler to take off thin strips, pulling toward me. When you can't get any more off the stalk, stop and save the rest for another use, like soup or risotto (page 59) tomorrow. Lift the carrots out of the brine and put them and the asparagus in a mixing bowl. Add most of the vinaigrette, the herbs, and ¼ teaspoon salt and use your hands to mix well, separating the ribbons of asparagus if they stick together. Taste, adjust, and arrange on a cool platter. Scatter the beets around and spoon over the remaining vinaigrette. Drape the salad with slices of gravlax (or pass it on a separate platter) and streak the top with crème fraîche.

* *A basket of broken-up pizza dough crackers (page 21) is nice to have at the table with this salad.*
* *As summer arrives, replace the asparagus with similarly sliced cucumbers.*

GRAVLAX

Cured salmon—gravlax—is a food that has one fin in the traditional peasant preservation kitchen and the other in fancy dining rooms. Humbly created as a way to keep an abundant catch from spoiling, it has become, like sisters salt cod and anchovy, a culinary staple. Just a heavy sprinkle of salt and sugar, those two magic powders, and this simple method of curing shows off salmon's fresh color and concentrates its oily lushness.

Makes about 1½ pounds

2 tablespoons salt

2 tablespoons sugar

2-pound wild salmon fillet, skin on, pin bones out

Freshly ground black pepper

4 dill sprigs (or basil, tarragon, cilantro, or mint)

In a small bowl, mix the salt and sugar. Cut the salmon fillet in half crosswise and grind a lot of black pepper over the flesh side of both pieces. Coat them with as much of the salt and sugar as will stick, rubbing the mixture in a little to make sure that every spot gets some, including the cut ends. Sandwich the fillets together, dill in the middle and skin sides out, place the bundle in a baking dish or shallow casserole, and cover it with a layer of plastic wrap or parchment paper. Place another dish or plate and a weight—a couple of cans of tomatoes or beans—on top. Refrigerate the salmon for 4 days, flipping it once a day. Do not be alarmed by the briny liquid that will appear around the fish—it is just that: a brine that your salmon is curing in. When flipping on the third day, give the thickest part a poke: you are looking for the flesh to feel set and firmer than when you started. If it still gives, the way it did when raw, sprinkle with a little more of the salt/sugar mixture. At the end of day 4, discard the brine and the herbs and give the fillets a quick rinse in cold water. Pat them dry and either start thinly slicing and eating—with cucumbers, brown bread, and cold aquavit, say—or wrap the fillets tightly and refrigerate them for up to a week.

GRILLED NEW ONIONS AND ARTICHOKES WITH ROMESCO SAUCE

I have never gone to a real *calçotada* in Spain, but *hombre*, do I ever want to! I want to drink wine while onions char in the fire, then steam and swipe them clean in bundles of newsprint. I want my shirt stained with chili-red romesco sauce and more of that *vino tinto* that helps me speak Spanish better. Or so it seems to me. Someday I will eat fire-roasted onions in Catalonia; till then, I'll grill and eat them here at home with chunky romesco sauce.

Makes 6 servings

½ lemon

6 artichokes

Salt

1 tablespoon good olive oil

1 tablespoon white or red wine vinegar

1 bay leaf

1 garlic clove, skin left on, cracked

¼ cup white wine (optional)

2 thyme sprigs (optional)

6 to 12 spring onions or 12 to 24 scallions (or, if neither are available, 1 or 2 large red onions, sliced into thick rings)

Cooking oil, olive or vegetable

A bowl of romesco (page 252)

Squeeze the lemon into a bowl of cold water big enough to hold the artichokes. Working from the bottom, snap the leaves off an artichoke until the lower third is pale green to yellow. Cut off the upper green part of the leaves and peel the base and stem with a paring knife or a vegetable peeler. If the stem is very tough, cut it, or part of it, off and then split the artichoke in half lengthwise. With a spoon, scoop out and discard the hairy choke, if any, and drop the artichoke into the lemon-water to prevent discoloring while you trim and cut the remaining artichokes the same way.

Drain the artichoke halves and discard the lemon-water. Put them into a saucepan, sprinkle with 1 teaspoon of the salt, and let them sit to absorb for a few minutes. Add the olive oil, vinegar, bay leaf, garlic, and, if you're using them, the wine and thyme. Add 1 teaspoon salt and just enough cold water to cover

the artichokes, then bring them to a boil over high heat. Lower the heat to bring them to a slow simmer and taste the water for salt, adding more if you can't taste it. Cook until the artichokes are tender, about 10 minutes. A paring knife should meet very little resistance when inserted into the heart of an artichoke. Drain and set them aside to cool.

Prepare a hot grill (see page 10).

Trim the hairy root ends and any brown or wilted parts from the onions and rinse them to get rid of grit. If you are using the bigger spring onions, split them in half lengthwise with a knife. Coat the onions and artichoke halves with cooking oil and sprinkle them with salt. When the coals are hot, place the artichokes cut side down on the grill, add the onions, and grill until the onions are cooked through and both the onions and artichokes are well marked. Arrange the vegetables on a warm platter and pass the romesco.

GREEN GARLIC BUDINO WITH ROASTED ASPARAGUS

This budino, like Japanese chawanmushi, is a delicate steamed custard. It is very simple to make, cooks quickly, and is versatile: everything from sesame oil to shrimp to truffles tastes good steamed in a budino. In spring, I like it especially with green garlic or leeks. In summer, a little tomato puree gives nice flavor and color. I have made them in the fall with roasted squash puree, and with winter greens when the cold weather makes greens sweeter. Chopped soft herbs like chives, parsley, chervil, or tarragon are great year-round.

You can steam little individual budini to unmold onto plates, or one larger one to scoop from at table. Either way, you have to rig up a way to steam them—I recommend a bamboo steamer, like for Chinese dumplings, or a cous-coussier.

Makes 6 servings

1 small leek, trimmed of dark green parts and root end cut off

1 stalk green garlic, trimmed of dark green parts and root end cut off

Cooking oil, olive or vegetable

Salt

1½ cups half-and-half

2 eggs

2 yolks

1¼ pounds asparagus, tough ends snapped off and (unless very thin) lower ⅔ of stalks peeled

¼ cup saffron or herb crème fraîche (page 249)

Leaves to garnish (see note, page 46)

Split the leek and green garlic in half lengthwise, then cut into ¼-inch slices and soak and swish well to get rid of any grit. Lift from the wash-water and put in a small skillet or saucepan with 3 tablespoons oil, ¼ teaspoon salt, and ¼ cup water. Bring to a simmer and cook gently until very tender, adding just enough water to keep from sizzling. Puree in a blender or food processor with ½ cup of the half-and-half until smooth. Set aside to cool.

Heat the oven to 450°F. Set up a steamer and bring the water in it to a boil.

In a mixing bowl, combine the eggs, yolks, the remaining 1 cup half-and-half, ¾ teaspoon salt, and the leek-garlic puree and whisk to combine. Divide among individual lightly oiled cups or ramekins or pour into a single oiled dish that can take steaming. Dress the asparagus with oil and salt and spread it on a baking sheet.

At the same time, put the asparagus in the oven and the budino dishes in the steamer. Cook the budino until set, 5 to 10 minutes, depending on size. The asparagus should be roasted tender in a similar time frame, again depending on size. Either one, if done before the other, can be removed from the heat and asked to wait for its partner. Spread the asparagus on a platter, spoon crème fraîche on top, and garnish with salad leaves. Serve warm with the budino.

Summer

EGGPLANT SALAD TWO WAYS

Eggplant boiled and braised, instead of my more typical grilled and fried, is a refreshing departure. A little stack of boiled baton salad next to one or two of the pan-roasted slices with a few leaves of rocket, cress, cilantro, basil, or mint scattered about is a nice nod to the summer garden.

Boiled Eggplant Batons with Lemon, Pine Nuts, and Mint

Makes 6 servings

Salt

1 large globe eggplant

1 small garlic clove, or ½ clove, pounded with a pinch of salt

1 tablespoon lemon juice

3 tablespoons good olive oil

Leaves from 6 mint sprigs, roughly chopped

2 tablespoons toasted pine nuts (page 9)

Put a medium pot of water on to boil. Add salt. Peel the eggplant and cut it into ½-inch slices, then cut the slices into ½-inch-wide strips. When the water is boiling and tastes nicely seasoned, add the eggplant and cook until tender, about 5 minutes. Drain well and set aside to cool.

Meanwhile make the vinaigrette: In a small bowl, mix together the pounded garlic, lemon juice, and a pinch of salt and let the mixture marinate for a few minutes, then stir in the oil.

Wrap the eggplant in a clean kitchen towel or doubled cheesecloth, squeeze out as much liquid as you can, and put it in a mixing bowl with the mint and pine nuts. Dress the salad with the vinaigrette and ¼ teaspoon salt and mix well. Taste, adjust, and let sit for 10 minutes to several hours at room temperature before serving.

Pan-Roasted Eggplant Slices with Cumin, Honey, and Sumac

Makes 6 servings

1 large globe eggplant

Salt

Cooking oil, olive or vegetable

2 garlic cloves, finely chopped

1½ teaspoons cumin seeds

Crushed red pepper flakes

1 tablespoon honey

Juice of ½ lemon

Good olive oil

1 teaspoon ground sumac

Using a vegetable peeler, peel strips lengthwise from the eggplant so that it is striped. Cut the eggplant into ½-inch-thick rounds and sprinkle with ¾ teaspoon salt. Heat a skillet to medium and add 3 tablespoons cooking oil and then as many eggplant slices as will fit in a single layer. Cook until they are browned, then turn them and brown the other sides, about 5 minutes per side. Set them aside, add more oil, and brown the remaining slices. Set aside.

Add 2 tablespoons cooking oil to the skillet and then the garlic, cumin seeds, and red pepper flakes. Stir until the garlic smells good and cooked, and before it browns at all, add ¾ cup water, the honey, and the lemon juice. Stir to melt the honey, then return the eggplant to the pan, crowding it so that the liquid bubbles around the slices. Simmer for 4 minutes, turn them over and simmer for 4 more. Check to be sure the eggplant is cooked through and fairly soft.

Turn the eggplant out onto a platter, drizzle with oil, sprinkle with the sumac, and let it cool to room temperature before serving.

FISH CARPACCIO WITH GINGERED CUCUMBERS, MELON, AND CUCUMBER GELÉE

I came out as a gelée enthusiast when I started calling it gelée instead of aspic. Gelée is fun to eat *and* fun to say, like "gel, eh?" Aspic is only fun to eat.

Easy to make from cucumbers, tomatoes, champagne, or flavorful broths, and served quaking atop cool fish or vegetable salads, gelée leaves no doubt that a dish is, in fact, fancy. In its analog way, gelée jiggles toward molecular cuisine, I suppose—or as close as my cooking gets. I like it especially with slices of raw, super-fresh fish, like fluke from the East Coast and yellowtail jack, king salmon, or California halibut out West.

Makes 6 servings

1¼ teaspoons gelatin

2 cucumbers (about 1¼ pounds)

Salt

1¼ teaspoons white wine vinegar

1 lime

1 teaspoon grated ginger (about ½ inch)

3 tablespoons good olive oil

½ favorite orange melon, peeled and seeded

Jalapeño to taste, seeded and finely diced

2 tablespoons chopped cilantro, and more nice leaves for garnish

12 to 14 ounces best fresh skinless fish fillet, trimmed of any bones and sinewy bits

In a small bowl, sprinkle the gelatin over ¼ cup cool water. Set aside to bloom.

Trim the ends from one of the cucumbers, cut it in half lengthwise, and then into ½-inch slices. Place in a blender with ½ teaspoon salt, ¼ teaspoon of the vinegar, juice of half the lime, and ½ cup cold water. Puree until very smooth, or until you can't stand it anymore, and then strain through a fine sieve, leaving the pulp to drain on its own and not pressing it—this gives a clearer, more enchanting Emerald City result. Taste and adjust the cucumber juice for salt and acidity. Gently warm the bowl of gelatin to melt it, but don't heat it too much—bring 1 inch of water to a simmer in a skillet, turn off the heat, and then dip the bottom of the bowl into the hot water. Stir the gelatin with your fingers until it's warm and you can no longer feel little gelled bits.

Mix ¼ cup of the cucumber juice into the gelatin, stir, and then pour the mixture into the cucumber juice and stir well. Into a flattish bowl, strain the mixture through a fine sieve to catch any undissolved gelatin. Refrigerate until set, about 2 hours. Chill the plates or platter for serving as well.

Meanwhile, make the dressing. In a small bowl, mix the ginger, the remaining 1 teaspoon vinegar, the juice of the other half of the lime, and ¼ teaspoon salt. Let sit for a few minutes, then stir in the oil.

When the gelée is set, peel the other cucumber, cut it in half lengthwise, and scoop out the seeds if they seem big and tough. Cut the melon into 1-inch-thick wedges. Thinly slice the cucumber and melon, and toss them with the jalapeño, chopped cilantro, most of the dressing, and a pinch of salt. Taste and adjust.

Thinly slice the fish across the grain and arrange it on chilled plates or a platter. Sprinkle each slice with a little salt, then spoon the cucumbers and melon on top. Spoon the rest of the dressing onto any fish that is yet undressed. With a paring knife, cut a crosshatch into the gelée and scoop out spoonfuls to wiggle over the plates. Quickly pick cilantro leaves to scatter over. Serve right away!

HAND-CUT PASTA WITH SQUID, BASIL, TOMATO, AND BREAD CRUMBS

Tender, egg-rich pasta is a wonderful thing in lasagna and so many other dishes, but sometimes I want a chewier noodle. Still tender, but also firm with a little bounce, kind of like udon or ramen. Using some water and a little less egg in this recipe gives a bit of chew, the soft double-zero flour keeps it tender, and the result is something like a cross between dried pasta and fresh. It mingles with this sauce of squid and tomatoes in a nicely wiggly way.

You do need a pasta machine to roll out this dough. If you didn't get one as a wedding present, be on the lookout for someone who did and is having a garage sale and giving up the fantasy that they will someday roll pasta. Look also at secondhand stores, or just buy a new one—they're not too pricey, especially if you get one without all the attachments that you don't need. I like my hand-cranked Atlas model.

Makes 6 servings

Salt

1 pound squid, cleaned and bodies cut into ½-inch rings (page 154)

3 tablespoons cooking oil, olive or vegetable

2½ cups summer marinara sauce (page 267)

1 batch double-zero pasta (recipe follows), cut linguine-width

2 tablespoons finely chopped parsley

Good olive oil

1 batch toasted bread crumbs (recipe follows)

Put a big pot of cold water on to boil. Add salt. When the water is nearly boiling, season the squid with salt and heat a skillet to high. Add the cooking oil to the skillet and then, carefully, the squid. In order to keep the skillet uncrowded, you may need to fry the squid in two batches. Watch out, squid spits as it fries. Let the squid cook for 2 minutes and then stir or toss it around to turn the pieces. When it is all lightly browned and no longer translucent,

2 to 3 minutes, lower the heat to medium and add the marinara sauce. Stir and scrape up any squid bits that are stuck. Add a splash of water if it seems too dry. Taste, adjust, and turn off the pan while you boil the pasta, stirring occasionally. When the pasta is cooked, after about 4 minutes, drain it and save ½ cup of the water in case the sauce needs thinning. Turn the heat under the sauce to medium-high, add the pasta, parsley, and some olive oil; stir well, taste, adjust, and serve hot sprinkled with toasted bread crumbs.

* *The squid can be replaced with fish cooked in olive oil (page 45) or with a can of nice tuna fish.*
* *Add a couple of spoonfuls of chopped olives and/or capers to the sauce.*
* *Double-zero pasta also works well with pesto, in Asian-flavored stir-fry, or with any tomato-based sauce.*

Double-Zero Pasta

Makes 6 small servings

1¼ cup 00 flour	1 teaspoon olive oil
1 egg	Pinch of salt

Measure the flour into a mixing bowl. In a separate bowl, whisk the egg, oil, salt, and ¼ cup water until completely mixed. Using a wooden spoon or your fingers, slowly stir the egg mixture into the flour. Use your hands to keep mixing the dough until it just holds together. It should be fairly crumbly, but add a little water if it's too dry to hold together. If it is sticky at all, knead in a little more flour.

Divide the dough into 4 or 5 lumps, shape them into balls, and then flatten them into discs. Set the discs on a plate, cover them with plastic and a kitchen towel, and leave them alone at room temperature for 1 hour or up to 4 hours.

Crank one of the discs of dough through the widest setting on your pasta machine. You may need to flatten it a bit with your hands or a rolling pin to get it started. Once it's through, if it seems at all sticky, sprinkle a little flour onto it, fold it in half, and roll it through again at the same setting. Keep folding and rolling until the dough becomes very even, smooth, and, ideally, neatly rectangular—six passes or so. Roll the rectangle up, tuck it back under the towel, repeat with the rest, and let them sit for half an hour, or a few hours if that suits you better.

Unroll one of the rectangles and feed it through the first setting again. Narrow the rollers to setting 2 and roll it through again. Continue on to setting 5 or 6, depending on how thick you like your pasta. Rolling through setting 5 twice kind of gives you a 5½, if that's your size. Sprinkle flour over the now long sheet of pasta and cut it into lengths that seem appropriate, about 8 inches. Making sure they are well floured, stack 2 sheets and, starting from a short end, roll them up together. With a sharp chef's knife, slice the roll thin for spaghetti, thicker for linguine, and so on. Detangle the spirals, sprinkling with flour as you toss them, and spread them, piled not too thickly, on a baking sheet or tray. Repeat with the remaining dough and refrigerate if you're not cooking right away. Depending on the thickness, fresh pasta will cook pretty quickly—4 to 5 minutes—in abundant, well salted, boiling water.

Toasted Bread Crumbs

Bread crumbs are best made from a loaf that is stale but not hard—fresh bread is too moist to crumble properly, and hard bread is too . . . hard (but can be ground finely and used for breading or meatballs/loaf). Both oily and dry crumbs keep for weeks in the refrigerator and can be recrisped if needed before use.

Makes about 3½ cups, plenty for a vegetable gratin (page 254),

romesco sauce (page 252), or for sprinkling on pasta (page 77).

Half a 1-pound rustic loaf, preferably a day or two old, crusts carved off

Good olive oil

Salt

Heat the oven to 350°F.

Cut or tear the bread into chunks and grind them coarsely in a food processor or blender. In a big bowl, combine the bread with ¼ cup oil and ½ teaspoon salt and mix well. The crumbs should be tasty and pretty oily, though not totally soaked. Add more oil or salt if needed, then spread the crumbs onto a baking sheet and bake for 7 minutes (set a timer). Using a spatula, scoop the crumbs into a pile, stir them around a bit, and spread them back out. Back into the oven for 5 minutes and repeat with the spatula. Keep baking and stirring, resetting the timer each time, until the crumbs are crisp and golden.

* *Sprinkle anywhere you want a savory crunch. Also nice with fried herbs (page 15) crumbled in.*

SLOW-BAKED SALMON WITH SHELL BEAN SALAD, SAGE, AND AÏOLI

This is really braised salmon, I suppose, but we always call it slow baked. Not sure why, although a chef I once cooked with did like to go slow and was often . . . Well, maybe he named it. A steamy 225°F oven renders the salmon just barely set, soft, and luxurious. If you have fig leaves or a friend somewhere who does and can slip a few in an envelope to you, they really do give a bewitching coconutty fragrance to the fish, and the room. A bed of sweet herbs like basil or mint might substitute. Rosemary is too strong here, but thyme and sage aren't.

Makes 6 servings

Freshly ground black pepper

1-pound salmon fillet

Salt

Cooking oil, olive or vegetable

2 fig leaves or a handful of sage stems

1 small garlic clove, pounded with ¼ teaspoon salt

2 teaspoons red wine vinegar

1 shallot

3 tablespoons good olive oil

1 red or orange Gypsy or bell pepper, seeded and thinly sliced

3 cups cooked fresh shell beans or cooked dried beans or chickpeas (2½ cups dried beans will make plenty for this recipe with some left over, which is good)

12 to 18 fried sage leaves (use the method on page 15)

Leaves to garnish (see note, page 46)

1 cup aïoli (page 265)

Heat the oven to 225°F. Grind black pepper over both sides of the salmon and sprinkle with 1 teaspoon salt. Let the fish sit for 10 to 15 minutes, then coat lightly with oil and set it on a rimmed baking sheet atop the fig leaves or herb stems. To avoid spillage, set the pan on the oven rack, then pour warm water into the pan to just cover the bottom. Bake until the salmon is still slightly translucent in the center, about 25 minutes. Set aside.

Meanwhile, in a medium bowl, mix the garlic paste, vinegar, shallot, and a sprinkling of ground pepper. Let marinate for a few minutes, then stir in the olive oil. In a large bowl, dress the pepper slices with a sprinkle of salt and most of the vinaigrette, so they can absorb and soften for a few minutes. Drain the beans—save the liquid—and add them to the pepper slices with most of the sage leaves, crumbled. Stir well, taste, and adjust. Add a splash of the bean liquid back in if you want more flow (any remaining liquid can be saved as a vegetable stock to use in soup-making).

When the fish is still warm, or just cooled, spread the bean salad on a platter and arrange chunks of salmon on top. Spoon the remaining dressing over the salmon, sprinkle with the rest of the fried sage leaves, and garnish with salad leaves. Pass a bowl of aïoli.

CORN SOUP WITH ROASTED RED PEPPER AND WILD MUSHROOMS

My friend Amy Dencler is one of the very best cooks I know—magic just seems to come from her sure hands. Not only does she make food beautiful, she also thinks some pretty deep thoughts about it, and it was Amy who suggested that we temper the natural sweetness of this corn soup with the acidity of some tomato. To keep the pale gold color, look for a yellow variety like Orange Blossom, Taxi, or Valencia.

Makes 6 servings

1 red bell pepper

5 ears corn

1 large ripe yellow or orange tomato

4 thyme sprigs, leaves roughly chopped, stems saved

6 parsley sprigs, leaves finely chopped, stems saved

1 bay leaf

Cooking oil, olive or vegetable

1 yellow onion, thinly sliced

Salt

¼ pound mushrooms, cleaned and sliced (wild chanterelles or morels are great; cultivated crimini are very good)

1 small garlic clove, chopped

¼ cup good olive oil

½ teaspoon red wine vinegar

Roast the pepper: Set it, as is, atop a gas burner turned up high. As each side chars, use tongs to turn to the next side until the skin is blackened all over. Put the pepper in a bag or covered container and set it aside to steam.

Make a cob stock: Peel the husks from the ears of corn and, using a towel or your hands, rub away as much of the silk as you can. Cut the kernels from the cobs and scrape them to get any flesh and juice left behind. Setting the cut kernels aside, snap the cobs in half and put them in a medium pot. Cut the tomato in half along the equator and gently squeeze out the seeds. Using the large holes of a box grater, grate the halves, on the cut side, into a bowl. Grate right down until all you have left is the skin—it won't go through the holes,

so you can really push it. Set the tomato pulp aside and add the skins to the pot with the cobs. Add the thyme and parsley stems, bay leaf, and 8 cups water and bring it to a boil over high heat. Lower the heat to a simmer and cook for 30 minutes. Strain the stock and discard the solids.

Meanwhile, heat a soup pot over high heat, add ¼ cup cooking oil and then the onion and 1 teaspoon salt. Stir, lower the heat, and cover the pot. Check and stir after a few minutes, letting the moisture collected on the lid drip back into the pot to keep things steamy. Lower the heat if there's any browning going on and re-cover. Cook like this until the onion is very tender, about 15 minutes. Add the corn kernels to the pot with another teaspoon of salt, the tomato pulp, and enough cob stock to cover them by 1 inch. You can always thin the soup later if it turns out too thick, so add just enough liquid to cover the vegetables and allow them to bob around a little. Bring the soup to a boil, turn it down to a simmer, and cook, stirring occasionally, until the corn is very tender, about 45 minutes.

While the soup is simmering, cook the mushrooms: Heat a skillet to high and add 2 tablespoons cooking oil and then the mushrooms and ¼ teaspoon salt. Toss to coat, and cook, stirring occasionally, until the mushrooms are browned and tender when tasted, about 10 minutes. Turn the heat to low and move the mushrooms to the sides of the pan. Add a little more oil if needed and the garlic and chopped thyme. Stir the garlic and thyme, and when they smell good, add the chopped parsley and stir everything together. Turn off the heat, add a splash of water to keep the garlic from browning, and leave to reheat later for garnishing.

When the soup is done, puree it: Working in batches, fill the blender less than halfway and, making sure to hold the lid on so hot soup doesn't spray the walls and you, puree until completely smooth. Add cob stock or water if it's too thick to really get going in the blender. Pour the soup through a sieve to catch any bits and ensure supersmoothness. Taste and correct for salt and texture, adding more water or cob stock if too thick. Rinse out the pot and return the soup to it for reheating.

Rinse out the blender to make the pepper puree. Peel the charred skin off the pepper with your fingers, pull off the stem end, and remove the seeds and membranes. Give the pepper a quick rinse, tear it into pieces, and put it in the blender with the olive oil, red wine vinegar, and a scant ¼ teaspoon salt. Puree until smooth and set aside.

Heat up the soup and the mushrooms if they've cooled. Ladle the soup into warm bowls, swirl with the red pepper puree, and sprinkle with the mushrooms.

EGGPLANT DORATO BAKED WITH TOMATO, BASIL, AND PARMESAN

In Italy they make fried chicken backwards, dipping breasts into flour and *then* egg before frying them up all *dorato*: golden. I like the way an omelet-y border haloes around the meat, and I like it especially with a summer tomato marinara sauce spooned over and crunchy fennel salad or boiled and oiled green beans alongside. Recently, I tried frying eggplant this way for some non-chicken-eating friends, spooning on the tomato sauce and then baking the whole thing with plenty of Parmesan and mozzarella. Herbivores and omnivores alike enjoyed it for its bubbly, cheesy richness, fresh, herby tomatocity, and satisfyingly meaty texture.

Makes 6 servings

2 large eggplants, weighing about 1 pound each

Salt

Cooking oil, olive or vegetable

Flour

2 eggs, beaten

Double batch (about 5 cups) summer marinara sauce (page 267), warmed

3 cups grated mozzarella (about ¾ pound)

1½ cups grated Parmesan (about ¼ pound)

Using a vegetable peeler, peel strips lengthwise from the eggplants so that they are striped. Cut them into ½-inch-thick slices, sprinkle them with salt, and set them aside for about 15 minutes to draw out some liquid.

Heat the oven to 400°F.

In a large skillet, heat ¼ inch of cooking oil to medium. Pat the eggplants dry and dredge in flour as many slices as will fit in a single layer in the skillet, coating both sides and shaking off the excess. Dip them into the beaten eggs, turn them to coat, and place them in the skillet. Adjust the heat so that they bubble nicely, and fry until one side is golden, 4 or 5 minutes; flip them over to fry the other side. Repeat with the next batch until they are all golden brown outside and tender in the middle.

Spread the warm marinara sauce into one or two baking dishes, arrange the eggplant slices over the sauce, and top them with the cheeses. Bake until they are very hot and the cheese is bubbling and golden, about 20 minutes. Serve the eggplant on its own as a first course, with a salad for lunch, or with a side of spaghetti tossed in a little more marinara sauce for an Italian-American retro dinner (seasoned to taste with checkered tablecloth, candle dripping down basketed Chianti bottle, Frank Sinatra on the jukebox . . .).

FIG AND SWEET PEPPER SALAD WITH MINT AND CRÈME FRAÎCHE

This simple salad can, when the ingredients are right, be a revelation. In fact, it's an embellishment on an even simpler salad that I learned, appropriately, from *Simple French Food* by Richard Olney, a book that has a kind of biblical standing at Chez Panisse. I may be, as a malaprop-popping friend used to say, gillying the lily by adding thin rings of sweet red peppers, but I do it for their crunch and color. Soft, ripe, sweet figs are what I call for here, but if yours are otherwise and you just gotta have it, quarter and roast them, tossed with oil and a pinch of salt, for 10 minutes or so first.

Makes 6 servings

5 mint sprigs	¼ cup crème fraîche (page 248)
1 teaspoon lemon juice	1 red or orange sweet pepper
1 teaspoon white wine vinegar	(Gypsy, Flamingo, Lipstick)
Freshly ground black pepper	Good olive oil
Salt	1 basket ripe figs, black or green

Crush 2 of the mint sprigs in your hands and put them in a small bowl with the lemon juice, vinegar, black pepper, and salt. Stir and let sit for 20 minutes to get the mint flavor in there. Pluck out the sprigs and discard. Set aside a teaspoon of the mixture. To the rest, add the crème fraîche and stir well.

Slice the sweet pepper into rings, as thin as you can. Trim the seeds and white membrane from the rings and dress them with the reserved lemon juice/vinegar, a pinch of salt, and enough oil to coat them. Toss and arrange on plates or a platter, a few rings per person. Cut some of the figs into lengthwise quarters and some into crosswise circles, and arrange them over the sweet pepper. Stripe the crème fraîche dressing over the figs and pepper, tear the remaining mint leaves, and scatter them over the salad. A final swirl of oil, a last sprinkle of salt and black pepper, and serve.

SUNGOLD TOMATO AND MELON SALAD WITH WHIPPED RICOTTA, BASIL, AND BLACK PEPPER

I love the fresh sheep's-milk ricotta I get from Bellwether Farms in Sonoma. It arrives bearing the thatch of the basket it was made in—so charming served in a slender slice alongside tomatoes and herbs, say, or fennel and orange slices, with plenty of good olive oil. And then I had an epiphany, a cheese epiphany: ricotta, when whipped, transforms. Like Jerry Lewis morphing from Julius Kelp to Buddy Love in *The Nutty Professor*, ricotta treated this way goes from endearingly nerdy and unkempt to irresistibly smooth and unctuous.

Makes 6 servings

4 basil sprigs

1 teaspoon white wine vinegar

1 teaspoon lemon juice

Freshly ground black pepper

Salt

12 ounces ricotta

Good olive oil

1 favorite melon, halved and seeds scooped out

1 basket Sungold or best cherry tomatoes, halved

2 to 4 scallions, all the white and most of the green parts, thinly sliced

3 or 4 radishes, thinly sliced

Crush a basil sprig with your fingers and put it in a small bowl with the vinegar, lemon juice, black pepper, and salt. Stir and then let sit for 20 minutes to get the basil flavor into the dressing.

Meanwhile, put the ricotta in a mixing bowl or food processor bowl. Whisk like crazy, or sanely push the button, until the ricotta becomes shiny and smooth, like very thick sour cream. Whisk in ¼ teaspoon salt and 2 tablespoons oil. Taste, adjust, and spoon the ricotta onto a platter in a big dollop and spread it out a little with the back of the spoon.

With another spoon, scoop out crescents of melon into a mixing bowl—depending on its size, you may not need the entire melon. Add the tomatoes, scallions, and radishes, tear basil leaves to toss in, and add ¼ teaspoon salt. Remove the basil sprig from the dressing and add 3 tablespoons oil. Stir well, add most of the dressing to the salad, and toss to coat.

Arrange the salad next to the ricotta, letting some of it overlap. Spoon the remaining dressing around and serve.

DOS GAZPACHOS

Years ago, when we were spending a chilly autumn in a beautiful, frigid Tuscan farmhouse, Kathleen and I took the three kids to Barcelona to warm up for a few days. The flight from Pisa was cheap enough that you wondered if it was even professional, but we went for it. Though the plane was shabby and flight attendants tried to sell us everything from scratch-off lottery tickets to bottles of perfume and Liam took a bite of a sandwich we'd grabbed at the airport and broke out in scary hives midflight from the mayonnaise he was (but isn't anymore, thank you) allergic to and we landed not in Barcelona but an hour's bus ride away, the trip was a success—and very delicious.

The first meal we had was at a truly down-home place, where wine was drawn from taps and only Catalan was spoken. We managed to order, in terrible Spanish, which wasn't even the waiter's language, a series of plates big and small. I was especially looking forward to the salt cod paella, and since my family did not share my enthusiasm for *bacalao*, I had it to myself. The first bite was wonderful, all salty saffron savor, but as I chewed, there was something else, something hard. A tooth, my tooth, was what it felt like, but surely it was a bone. Yes, a cod bone, a vertebra, had to be. How rustic, I mused, smiling and sucking the salty fish from the bone. The feeling I had when I spit it, discreetly, into my hand and saw that it was, in fact, a tooth and—a quick check with the tongue confirmed—not my own, was plain horror. It was a big yellow molar that *looked human*! My smile did not fade, it was snuffed out, and my family was concerned. I hid the truth, the ugly tooth, from them, trying to limit the damage, trying to not think about who was stirring the paella when his old tooth fell into it, trying not to think of something worse.

I motioned to the waiter.

"What is it?" my wife asked.

"Something. From the paella. In my mouth."

"Well, you have to tell us what it is, or we'll imagine something really awful."

I motioned to the waiter.

"I found this," I said in the English I knew he didn't understand, supplemented with the gestures that he clearly did, "in the paella."

I held out the tooth, and someone gasped. It wasn't the waiter, who, losing his battle to not smile, turned and fled to the kitchen. We heard Catalan laughter. The waiter returned with another smile-suppressing waiter who spoke English and explained that the tooth belonged to a pig, or it had until stock was made from the pig's head and that stock was used in the *paella de bacalao*. And then that tooth ended up in my head, I didn't bother saying.

That one of the other dishes we'd ordered was pig cheek comforted me—it made sense that pig heads were present in the kitchen. I drank long from my glass, which helped me settle on the only realistic option: to believe what he said and to eat no more paella at this restaurant.

"Maybe I should have ordered gazpacho," I grumbled. The waiter turned, fluent for a flash, my regional culinary ignorance enlightening him.

"Gazpacho," he said in accented but understandable English, "it is a dish from Andalusia, *senyor—aquí*, you are in Catalunya!"

Cucumber and Watermelon Gazpacho with Almonds and Basil

Cucumbers and watermelon, very cool individually, achieve a state of refreshment when they are combined that is greater than the sum of its parts. Savory, a little sweet, and frosty pale, this is a soup for deep summer.

Makes 6 servings

¼ cup raw almonds

2 cucumbers, peeled

2 cups seedless watermelon chunks (about ¼ small watermelon)

2 scallions or 1 spring onion, all the white and most of the green parts, thinly sliced

¼ cup basil leaves

Good olive oil

1 cup torn crustless bread

1 lemon

Salt

This dish has two parts: the smooth pureed soup and the crunchy salsa garnish. When making the soup part, save a little of the cucumber, melon, scallions, and basil to dice small for the garnish part.

Bring a small pot of water to a boil, add the almonds, and turn off the heat. After 15 seconds, dip out a small handful of almonds and squeeze them one by one to slip off the skins. Repeat with the remaining almonds—the skins come off easier if they are left in the hot water until you are ready. Put the almonds in a medium bowl and, using the large holes of a box grater, grate most of the cucumbers into the bowl. Add most of the melon, scallions, and basil, ¼ cup oil, the bread, the juice of half the lemon, and ½ cup cold water, stir well, and let sit while the bread softens, stirring once or twice, about 15 minutes. Spin the soup in batches in a blender until very smooth. Pass through a sieve for extra textural advantage. Taste, adjust, and chill well.

Cut the reserved cucumber and melon into small dice and toss in a bowl with the reserved sliced scallions, torn basil leaves, and a pinch of salt. Dress with a squeeze of lemon juice and a generous glug of oil. Taste, adjust, and when the soup is cold, ladle it into chilled bowls and top each with a spoonful of the salsa.

* *Serve with tomato gazpacho (recipe follows), ladling the two soups into the bowl simultaneously for a half-and-half effect.*
* *Substitute mint or cilantro for the basil and add finely diced jalapeños to the salsa.*

Tomato Gazpacho with Paprika, Toasted Bread Crumbs, and Tarragon

Here, earthy paprika and licorice-y tarragon deepen the sweet summer tomato. This dish has two parts: the smooth pureed soup and the crunchy salsa garnish.

Makes 6 servings

1 cucumber, peeled

2 pounds ripe red tomatoes, cored

2 scallions or 1 spring onion, thinly sliced

½ teaspoon chopped tarragon

1 cup torn crustless bread

1 garlic clove, pounded with a pinch of salt

1 tablespoon sweet paprika or other ground sweet red chili, plus more for the garnish

¼ cup good olive oil, plus more for the garnish

1½ teaspoons salt, plus more for the garnish

1½ teaspoons red wine vinegar, plus more for the garnish

⅓ cup toasted bread crumbs (page 79)

Using the large holes of a box grater, grate most of the cucumber into a mixing bowl. Cut the tomatoes in eighths and add all but a few of them to the cucumber. Stir in all the remaining ingredients except for the toasted bread crumbs, reserving a little of the scallions and tarragon. Add ½ cup cold water and let the mixture sit for 15 minutes, stirring once or twice. Spin the soup in batches in a blender until very smooth. Pass through a sieve for extra textural advantage. Taste, adjust, and chill well.

Dice the reserved cucumber and tomatoes and put in a bowl with the reserved sliced scallions and chopped tarragon, a pinch of salt, and a couple of pinches of paprika. Stir in a little splash of red wine vinegar and a generous glug of oil. Taste and adjust. Ladle the cold soup into chilled bowls, top each with a spoonful of the salsa, sprinkle with bread crumbs, and serve.

* *Add ⅓ cup cooked crabmeat or boiled and sliced shrimp to the salsa.*

Fall

GRILLED CHANTERELLE MUSHROOMS WITH GREMOLATA, CRÈME FRAÎCHE, AND CORNCAKES

Imagine that, as if in a folk tale, you skip into the woods one dewy morning to meet the woodcutter for a picnic. Along the way, the wolf eats your lox, leaving your basket of warm corncakes and cold champagne incomplete. Though sad, you're grateful that you yourself were not eaten, and hurry on to your rendezvous, but not so quickly that you don't pause to pick a few of the golden chanterelles that hide beneath the spreading oaks along the path. A plan for lunch begins to form in your clever head. Fortunately, while you were delayed, your able woodcutter lit a little fire of wood chips and fragrant branches. You follow smoke to fire and once the flames have subsided and the coals are aglow, it all falls into place, and right there in the forest, you get to cooking.

Makes 6 servings

½ cup all-purpose flour

½ cup cornmeal

2 teaspoons baking soda

Salt

1 egg

¾ cup milk

4 tablespoons (½ stick) unsalted butter, melted

4 scallions, all of the white and most of the green parts, thinly sliced

1 tablespoon chopped parsley

½ garlic clove, very finely chopped

1 teaspoon grated lemon zest

1 pound chanterelle mushrooms (or porcini, crimini, button, or king trumpet), trimmed and cleaned

Cooking oil, olive or vegetable

3 tablespoons crème fraîche (page 248), room temperature

Water or milk, if needed

Light the grill and while it gets hot, make the corncake batter: In a medium bowl, mix the flour, cornmeal, baking soda, and ½ teaspoon salt. Mix the egg with the milk and stir into the flour mixture until fully combined, then add 2 tablespoons of the melted butter and the scallions. Stir well and set aside.

To make the gremolata, mix the parsley, garlic, and lemon zest in a small bowl and set it aside.

Cut the mushrooms into halves or quarters if they're too big to grill whole and toss them with a sprinkling of salt and enough cooking oil to coat well. Heat the oven to warm for holding the mushrooms or corncakes once cooked. Thread the mushrooms on skewers if you like, and when the fire is ready, grill them (or ask your friend to grill while you make the corncakes; leave a trail of gremolata so she can find her way home).

Heat a skillet to medium, add a coating of cooking oil, and add spoonfuls of the batter. Flip the corncakes when bubbles begin to form in the middles, cook the other side, and then hold them on a platter in the warm oven while you cook the rest.

Arrange the corncakes on the warm platter, spoon the remaining warm melted butter on top, and scatter the grilled mushrooms around. Stripe the top with the crème fraîche, thinned with water or milk if needed to make it pourable, sprinkle with the gremolata, and live happily ever after.

ASIAN PEAR AND FENNEL SALAD WITH FRICO

Asian pears are among Liam's favorite fruits. I appreciate their exotic floral flavor and strangely granular succulence, but I wondered what he liked so much about them. "Juishy," he gushed through a mouthful, "and sho shweet and crunshy!" When tossed with shaved fennel and fried sage leaves, and served with salty Parmesan frico, I'd add "shurprishingly shavory!"

Makes 6 servings

1 tablespoon fennel seeds

Salt

Sugar

Apple cider vinegar

¼ cup white wine or water

1 small shallot, finely diced

Freshly ground black pepper

3 tablespoons good olive oil

1 large fennel bulb, trimmed and halved top to bottom

2 large Asian pears

⅓ cup parsley leaves, whole if tender and small, otherwise chopped coarsely

20 fried sage leaves (use the method on page 15)

12 frico (page 26)

Pickle the fennel seeds: Combine them in a small saucepan with 1 teaspoon each salt, sugar, and cider vinegar and the white wine or water. Bring to a boil, turn off the heat, and let cool.

In a small bowl, mix the shallot, ¼ teaspoon salt, 2 teaspoons vinegar, and black pepper and let marinate for a few minutes. Stir in the oil and set aside.

Using a chef's knife or mandoline, slice the fennel crosswise, as thinly as you can. Stop when you get to the core, or keep slicing if it seems tender. Set the fennel aside in a medium bowl and quarter the pears, core the quarters, and cut them into ⅛-inch-thick slices. Put the pears in the bowl with the fennel and add the parsley, drained pickled fennel seeds, and most of the dressing. Crumble in half of the sage leaves, mix well, taste, adjust, and spread on a platter. Spoon the extra dressing on top, and break up 6 of the frico to scatter over the salad with the remaining sage leaves. Pass the rest of the frico at the table.

BUTTERNUT SQUASH PANADE WITH RED WINE, THYME, AND GRUYÈRE

Panade is like lasagna made with bread in the layers instead of pasta. I learned to make it from my friend and former co-chef, Russ Moore. Russ has his own place now, where he grills nearly everything, and the rest he roasts in the wood oven, but back in the Chez Panisse days, he used to make panade. It was kind of a hard sell at first—no one really got what it was, which might have been part of what Russ liked about it. He'd layer butternut squash sliced thin with crisp toasted levain bread and red winey, thyme-speckled onions, and then bake the whole thing with hot chicken stock and a crust of Gruyère cheese. After a finish in the wood oven, it was browned and bubbling hot, and when the sweet, smoky aroma made its way through the dining room, people got it.

Makes 6 servings with ample leftovers

1 large loaf stale rustic bread (about 1½ pounds)

Cooking oil, olive or vegetable

Salt

Butter

2 yellow onions, thinly sliced

6 to 8 thyme sprigs, leaves picked from stems and chopped (about 2 tablespoons)

½ bottle red wine (about 1½ cups)

2½-pound butternut squash

6 cups chicken stock (page 44)

1½ cups grated Gruyère (about 6 ounces)

Heat the oven to 350°F.

Slice the bread as thinly as possible (this is where staleness helps—a fresh loaf is difficult to slice thinly). Sprinkle oil onto a baking sheet, then lay out the slices. They won't all fit, so you can use 2 sheets or work in batches. Sprinkle or brush the slices with more oil and a little salt and shuffle the slices, rubbing them together and soaking up whatever oil is on the pan. Rearrange the slices so they're all in a single layer again and toast them for 7 minutes. Turn the pan front to back and toast for a few more minutes, if necessary, resetting your timer each time, until the toasts are golden brown all over with no pale patches. The toasts will probably not all be done at the same time, so remove the ones that are, and keep toasting (timer!). Break off any parts that seem too dark and set the toasts aside.

Meanwhile, heat a skillet to high and add 2 tablespoons oil, 2 tablespoons butter, and then the onions and ½ teaspoon salt. Stir occasionally until things get going, then turn the heat to low. Cook, stirring from time to time, until the onions are very soft and lightly browned, about 20 minutes—adding a splash of water now and then helps. Add the thyme and stir and cook for a minute, then add the wine, raise the heat, and cook until the wine has reduced by half.

With a vegetable peeler, peel the squash. Cut it in half across, just above where it swells, so you have a flat side to set it on. Cut the round part in half and scoop out the seeds and membranes. Cut the squash in thin slices, about ¼ inch thick. Bring the chicken stock to a boil and start building the panade. Brush a 3-quart baking dish, casserole, or a large cast-iron pan with oil, then fit in a layer of bread, breaking the slices up if necessary to fill in gaps. Arrange a third of the squash slices over the bread and sprinkle them with salt and a third of the winey onions. Repeat until there are 4 layers of bread and 3 of filling.

Pour the hot stock over the panade, cover it with foil, and bake until the squash is cooked, about 45 minutes. Use a thin knife blade to check for doneness—it should meet no resistance from the squash slices. Uncover the panade and dot with butter. Return it to the oven until it is browned on top, 25 to 30 minutes. Sprinkle the top with cheese, raise the heat to 450°F, and bake another 10 to 15 minutes to get it bubbly and brown. The panade should be quite wet under the top crust, almost soupy. Add hot stock if needed to make it so. Cut it into squares or simply spoon it out of the dish to serve.

* *Instead of thyme and red wine, stir a couple of tablespoons curry spice mix (in descending amounts: coriander, cumin, turmeric, fennel, mustard, paprika, ginger, clove . . . something spicy if you like) and a little handful of chopped cilantro stems and leaves into the onions. Skip the cheese or, quirkily, don't.*
* *Serve as a first course, like soup, or alongside meat, poultry, or a nice poached egg.*

FARRO AND ESCAROLE SALAD WITH POMEGRANATE, PANCETTA, CILANTRO, AND AGED GOAT CHEESE

I like to make this salad with nearly as much farro as escarole, so depending how big your head is—of escarole, I mean—you may not need the whole thing. Save some leaves for sandwiches. Nice as a first course and pretty picnicky alongside grilled chicken or lamb or especially, if you are so lucky as to be able to find some, grilled young goat. Seriously.

Makes 6 servings

Salt

1 cup farro

Good olive oil

Cooking oil, olive or vegetable

2 or 3 thick slices pancetta (about 6 ounces; page 53), cut across into little strips

1 shallot, diced tiny

1 tablespoon red wine vinegar

2 teaspoons sherry vinegar

Freshly ground black pepper

1 head escarole, leaves trimmed of dark green tips, cut from the core, washed, and dried

Seeds of a medium pomegranate (about 1 cup)

Small handful cilantro sprigs, stems chopped finely, leaves coarsely, plus a few whole sprigs for garnish

2 ounces aged firm goat cheese, such as Garrotxa, Gouda, or Impromptu from Andante Dairy

Bring a medium pot of water to a boil and add salt and the farro. Lower the heat so that it bubbles, but not a lot, and cook until the farro is tender, with a little bite, about 30 minutes (some farro can take much longer—taste it to determine doneness and add water if it's reducing too much). Drain, sprinkle with olive oil, stir to coat, and set aside to cool.

Meanwhile, heat a small skillet to medium and add ½ tablespoon cooking oil and the pancetta. Cook, stirring occasionally, until the pancetta is transparent and browning on the edges, or until crispy, if you prefer, but don't let it get too dark or the rendered fat will taste burned, and you want some for the vinaigrette. Drain and set the pancetta and fat aside.

In a small bowl, combine the shallot, vinegars, pepper, and salt and allow to marinate for a few minutes. Stir in 5 tablespoons olive oil and 1 of the pancetta fat. Taste, adjust, and set aside.

Line up a handful of escarole leaves on a cutting board and slice them into ¼-inch shreds. Repeat with the remaining escarole and toss it in a salad bowl with the farro, pomegranate seeds, pancetta, chopped cilantro, salt, pepper, and most of the vinaigrette. Mix well with your hands, taste, and adjust. Serve in the bowl or piled on a platter, sprinkled with the remaining vinaigrette, shavings of goat cheese, and cilantro leaves.

* *Replace the pancetta with ½ cup toasted and chopped walnuts (see page 9), and the pancetta fat in the vinaigrette with an extra tablespoon good olive oil.*
* *Replace the goat cheese with smoked duck breast: Prepare and season one or two duck breasts as described in duck cooked two ways (page 172), rubbing a teaspoon of brown sugar onto the duck in addition to the salt and spices. Let sit for 15 minutes, then cook in an oiled skillet on the skin side only, over medium heat, until the fat is well rendered and the skin is browned. You're not trying to cook the duck through—that will happen while smoking—but rather to achieve browned crispy skin over cooked luxurious fat, so . . . not too fast (browned skin, but unrendered fat) or too slow (fat rendered, but skin pale and soft). Get the heat right so that the skin is coloring and a lot of fat is accumulating in the pan—signs of proper rendering. When the skin is mahogany and much of the fat has melted away, remove the breast and smoke as for fish (page 133), until the meat is set and firm, but still pink in the middle. Let cool, then slice thinly to serve with the salad.*

MAGIC PUMPKIN CARAMELLE WITH WILD NETTLES AND SWEET RED CHILI

We used to have an old Volvo sedan, the kind that is simultaneously boxy and roundy and further defies physics by somehow seeming much larger on the inside than the outside. It was Halloween orange, faded, and peeling a little from the Oakland sun. I bought the car from a sweet guy, a performer who recorded songs for kids, and when we made the deal, he threw in a copy of his latest CD, *I Like Noodles (yes, I doodle!)*, which, after but one listen, wormed so deep into my ear that it noodles there still. The car had a name, of course, and that stuck too: the Magic Pumpkin. The old thing ran great, and every year, when trick-or-treating time came around, I'd give the kids jars of black tempera and tell them to paint my car. Once they saw that I was serious, the neighbor kids joined in, and it was a beautiful and frightening sight—naughty and deviant, and it washed off in a week.

Though this dish is named after our Magic Pumpkin car, actual pumpkins mostly tend to cook up too wet and washed out for ravioli filling. I prefer kabocha or Buttercup squashes. One of my favorite growers, Full Belly Farm in Yolo County, grows some amazing little rust-colored, dense-fleshed squashes called Honeynut that are so cute and sweet they put a charm on us every autumn—if you find some, buy them, and you'll fall under their spell as well.

This filling is wonderful for making other shapes like ravioli or tortellini of course, but caramelle, looking like little wrapped candies, seem like the right shape for Halloween season.

Makes 6 servings

1 small winter squash (about 1 pound)

Salt

Cooking oil, olive or vegetable

7 tablespoons unsalted butter

Crushed red pepper flakes (optional)

⅓ cup grated Parmesan, plus additional Parmesan to grate at the table

2 tablespoons sweet chili powder (about 4 whole dried chilies or 1 ounce—see harissa, page 261, for more on this)

1½ teaspoons red wine vinegar

1 batch egg pasta dough (page 146)

½ pound nettles or spinach, large stems removed

Good olive oil

Heat the oven to 450°F.

Carefully cut the squash in half from top to bottom and scoop out the seeds and stringy stuff. Season the cut sides with ½ teaspoon salt and rub them with oil. Place the halves cut side up on a baking sheet, cover loosely with foil, and roast until very soft, about 45 minutes to an hour. Times will vary with squash size and variety, so test for doneness by inserting a paring knife—it should meet with no resistance. Remove the squash from the oven, and when it's cool enough to handle, use a large spoon to scoop the flesh out. Crank it through a food mill, spin it in the food processor, or stir it vigorously with a whisk to puree. If the resulting puree seems wet, spoon it into the middle of a clean kitchen towel or double layer of cheesecloth, twist it into a ball, and squeeze out as much liquid as you can. Turn the squash out into a mixing bowl.

Put 3 tablespoons of the butter in a small saucepan or skillet and heat on high. The butter will melt, then foam, then begin to brown. When it is colored around the edges and smelling nutty, add the red pepper flakes, if using, and then quickly pour the mixture into the squash puree. Add the ⅓ cup grated Parmesan, stir well, taste, adjust, and set aside.

Make the chili sauce: Put the chili powder in a small mixing bowl, add a scant ¼ cup hot water, stir, and set it aside for 30 minutes to hydrate and become a paste. Melt the remaining butter and add it, the red wine vinegar, and ¼ teaspoon salt to the sauce. Stir well, taste, adjust, and set aside.

Using a pasta maker, start rolling out the pasta, making it incrementally thinner until it is just translucent, about the thickness of heavy paper or cardstock. On my machine, this is number 6. Because pasta dough doesn't always behave the same way, I sometimes roll the dough through 6 twice, if I want it thinner, but not so thin as number 7. On a floured surface, cut the long sheet of pasta into shorter lengths of about 16 inches. Keep one to work with first, sprinkle the rest with flour, stack them, and set them aside, covered so that they don't dry out.

Brush any loose flour off the sheet you're starting with and cut it in half lengthwise so that you have 2 strips about 3 inches wide. Lightly brush or spritz the strips with water so they will seal when folded. Using a pastry bag or small spoon, place elongated teaspoonfuls of the filling along the center of the strips in rows. Leave 1½ inches between each portion of filling and you should be able to fit 5 on each strip. Fold the pasta toward you and over the filling, and starting at one end so that the air can escape from the other, smooth the dough around the lumps of filling. Your fingers should slide over the pasta as you go—if the pasta is grabbing and wrinkling, dip your fingers in flour before you curve them around each filling bump. When both strips are sealed, use a sharp knife to trim the long sides where the edges meet, leaving a border between filling and edge of about ¼ inch. Cut between the filling with your sharp knife or, if you have one, a zigzag pasta cutter. Turn the caramelle onto their fat bellies, ridges up, and pinch the ends so that they are crumpled and candy-wrapper-like. Repeat to use up all of the filling and set the finished caramelle on floured trays, making sure that they do not touch each other, or they will stick. Refrigerate if not cooking soon.

Bring a big pot of water to a boil and add salt. The nettles or spinach will cook in the same time as the caramelle, about 5 minutes, so heat a skillet to medium, then slip the caramelle into the boiling water, lowering the heat so it continues to boil, but more gently. Add 2 tablespoons cooking oil to the skillet and then the greens and a pinch of salt. Stir the caramelle gently so as not to break

them, and stir the greens as well. Lower the heat under the greens to wait for the caramelle, and when they are done, dip them out of the water and into the skillet. Toss with care, adding a glug of olive oil for shine, and turn them out onto a warm platter or into a wide bowl. You can spoon the chili sauce over, but it tends to redden everything alarmingly, so maybe it's better to pass at the table with Parmesan for grating.

* *If you are so skilled and lucky as to make more caramelle than you need for now, the overage freezes well and can go straight from freezer to boiling pasta pot when you're ready.*

ROASTED ROOT AND FRISÉE SALAD WITH DUCK CONFIT AND RED PEPPER VINAIGRETTE

Though not a big offal eater, I do like chopped liver, provided it's half butter and has plenty of herbs and wine; and poultry hearts and gizzards, especially when spiced and seasoned and cooked slowly in duck fat: confit. If chicken, duck, or turkey hearts or gizzards are not available, duck leg confit, or even chicken leg confit, will work shredded up with this salad as well. This is a good one to make on the seasonal cusp between summer and fall, when all the root vegetables are coming to markets and sweet red peppers are still around.

Makes 6 servings

1 small red bell pepper or other sweet pepper such as Corno di Toro or Jimmy Nardello

1 garlic clove, pounded with ¼ teaspoon salt

½ teaspoon cumin seeds, toasted and ground (page 9)

2 teaspoons red wine vinegar

1½ teaspoons sherry vinegar

1 shallot, finely diced

Salt

¼ cup good olive oil

1 pound root vegetables, such as carrots, parsnips, rutabagas, celery root, turnips, Jerusalem artichokes, and radishes (a combination is festive)

2 tablespoons cooking oil, olive or vegetable

About 10 ounces duck, turkey, or chicken hearts and gizzards confit, sliced (page 117), or 1 duck leg confit, shredded off the bone

2 frisée heads, trimmed of dark green or wilted parts, leaves cut from the heart, washed and spun dry

Freshly ground black pepper

1 tablespoon chopped parsley or mint or both

Roast the pepper by setting it, as is, atop a gas burner turned up high. As each side chars, use tongs to turn to the next side until the skin is blackened all over. Put the pepper in a bag or covered container and set it aside to steam.

Heat the oven to 450°F.

In a medium bowl, mix the garlic paste, cumin, vinegars, and shallot and set aside.

When the pepper has cooled, peel the charred skin off with your fingers, pull off the stem end, and remove the seeds and membranes. Give it a quick rinse and, in the blender or food processor, finely grind but don't quite puree it with ¼ teaspoon salt. Add to the shallot mixture, stir in the olive oil, taste, adjust, and set aside.

Peel the root vegetables and cut them into batons or wedges. If you are using a combination of different roots, pay attention to their densities as you cut them: the harder vegetables will take longer to cook through, so you'll want to cut them a bit smaller and make the more tender ones a bit thicker. Toss them in a bowl with the cooking oil and ½ teaspoon salt and toss well to coat. Spread on a baking sheet and roast until browned and tender, 15 to 20 minutes, stirring them only if they're getting too dark on the bottom. Turn the roots out into a salad bowl; spread the sliced and shredded confit on the vacated baking sheet and put it in the oven to heat for 5 minutes.

Mix the frisée with the vegetables, a sprinkle of salt, black pepper, and most of the vinaigrette. Taste, adjust, and transfer to a platter, scatter with the duck confit and the chopped herbs, and spoon over the remaining vinaigrette.

* *Lightly peel, seed, and cut a Delicata squash into ½-inch slices to roast dressed with oil and salt (together with the roots, if there's room on the sheet, or separately).*
* *Instead of duck confit, scatter rendered and lightly crisped bacon or pancetta bits or toasted and chopped almonds or pistachios over the salad.*
* *Replace some or all of the frisée with escarole, curly endive, or radicchio. A handful of arugula mixes in well.*

DUCK CONFIT WITH FENNEL SEED

I do insist that you season the duck the day before you plan to cook it. I don't insist, but do recommend, that you cook it a few days or up to a month before you plan to eat it—it gains interest like money in the bank.

This recipe is for two legs; it is always good to have a duck leg up your sleeve.

Makes 2 duck legs

2 teaspoons fennel seeds, toasted and ground (see page 9)

Freshly ground black pepper

Crushed red pepper flakes

4 bay leaves

1½ teaspoons salt

2 duck legs (about 10 ounces each), or same amount of poultry hearts or gizzards

1½ cups rendered duck fat

The day before cooking, combine the spices and salt and sprinkle the mixture onto the duck legs. Cover and refrigerate them overnight.

Bring the legs to room temperature. Melt the duck fat over medium heat in a saucepan that will fit the duck legs without too much extra room. Slip the legs into the fat, bring it to a simmer. Lower the heat so the fat just murmurs around the submerged legs. Cook until very tender, about 1½ hours. To check for doneness, grab the drumstick bone with tongs and the end of the thighbone with your other hand and a kitchen towel. Bend the ends toward each other, and if it feels like you could easily make them touch, it's done. If the joint still feels springy, cook the legs more. Let the legs and fat cool separately.

To store the duck, place it in a snug container and ladle fat over to completely cover it. Stop ladling before you reach the liquid that lurks beneath the fat—it's tasty, if salty, but will cause the duck to spoil if stored with it (the liquid can be used, with awareness of its salinity, for soup-making). Duck confit will keep, refrigerated and completely fat-covered, for a month at least.

When you're ready to eat a leg, pull it from the fat and shred the meat off the bone or crisp the whole thing, mostly on the skin side, in a cast-iron pan.

PORCINI MUSHROOM SOUP WITH CORIANDER, CELERY, AND MINT

I first made this soup during an especially wet winter that brought up an embarrassment of porcini mushrooms. I forage them myself and that year was in enviable possession of too many of those plump kings of the forest. The mushrooms, as they are, don't take well to freezing, but it occurred to me that mushroom soup might, as indeed it does. When the California forests are too dry for wild mushrooms to appear, I make soup from cultivated crimini mushrooms instead, and it is very nearly as good.

Makes 6 servings

4 tablespoons cooking oil, olive or vegetable

4 tablespoons (½ stick) butter

1 yellow onion, thinly sliced

Salt

1½ pounds porcini or crimini mushrooms, cleaned and sliced

2 garlic cloves, chopped

2 tablespoons dry sherry or ¼ cup white wine

1 small russet potato (about 6 ounces), peeled, halved lengthwise, and sliced ½ inch thick

7 cups chicken stock (page 44) or part stock, part water

1 cup thinly sliced celery (2 to 3 stalks)

1 teaspoon lemon juice

½ teaspoon grated lemon zest

1 teaspoon coriander seeds, toasted and ground coarsely (see page 9)

2 tablespoons chopped mint leaves

Good olive oil

Heat a soup pot over high heat and add 2 tablespoons of the cooking oil, 2 tablespoons of the butter, and, when it stops foaming, the onion and 1 teaspoon salt. Stir, turn the heat to low, and cover the pot. Check and stir after a few minutes, letting the moisture collected on the lid drip back into the pot to keep it steamy. Lower the heat if there's any browning going on, and re-cover. Cook like this until the onion is very tender, about 15 minutes, adding a splash of water as needed.

Meanwhile, heat a large skillet to high, add 1 tablespoon of the cooking oil and 1 tablespoon of the butter and, when it stops foaming, half of the mushrooms and ½ teaspoon salt. Cook, stirring occasionally and lowering the heat if necessary, until nicely browned, about 5 minutes. Set them aside while you cook the remaining mushrooms the same way, using the remaining 1 tablespoon oil and 1 tablespoon butter and adding the garlic right at the end of the second batch. Cook for half a minute, taking care to not burn the garlic, then return the first batch of mushrooms to the skillet. Add the sherry or white wine and let simmer for a minute before turning off the heat.

When the onion is done, add the cooked mushrooms and any juices to the pot along with the potato and stock. Bring to a boil, reduce to a simmer, stir once or twice, and cook for 30 minutes. Let cool a little, then—working carefully and in batches—puree until very smooth in a blender. Taste, adjust, and return the soup to the pot.

While the soup is cooking, bring a small pot of salted water to a boil and add the celery. Cook until tender, about 5 minutes, then drain and cool to room temperature. In a small bowl, combine the celery, ¼ teaspoon salt, the lemon juice and zest, the coriander, mint, and 3 tablespoons olive oil, mix well, taste, and adjust.

Rewarm the soup as needed, ladle it into warm bowls, and spoon the celery salsa on top. A final swirl of olive oil is nice.

BITTER GREENS PANSOTTI WITH SALSA DI NOCI

The filling for these big pot-bellied ravioli is made with any kind of cooked greens, but bitter ones like radicchio, curly endive, escarole, frisée, or dandelion should be at least included, if not featured (you don't need to use whole heads of tender greens that might otherwise be salad: the trimmings—leaves that are too tough, or the greener parts of frisée, endive, and escarole—can be cooked to tenderness with a little water, oil, and enough time). Spinach, arugula, broccoli rabe, even some sorrel, purslane, or nettles if you can find them, are nice as well—a mixture of greens makes for a more interesting pansotto. The very green-and-leanness of the filling can seem stark, but it's good that way—on the plate, the rich, oily salsa di noci surrounds and soothes any bitterness.

Makes 6 servings

1 pound greens for cooking (see above for suggestions)

¼ cup cooking oil, olive or vegetable

¼ teaspoon salt

1 garlic clove, finely chopped

½ cup ricotta

¼ cup grated pecorino or Parmesan, plus more to grate when serving

2 tablespoons good olive oil

½ teaspoon lemon juice or vinegar

1 batch egg pasta dough (page 146)

Salsa di noci (page 270)

Remove any tough stems from your greens, give them a rough chop, just once through with the knife, and drop them into a big bowl of cold water. Swish them around to get rid of any dirt and dip them out into a colander (don't pour them out or the dirt will just go right back on), but do not spin dry—it's good to have some water clinging to the leaves to help them steamily cook. Heat a skillet to medium and add the cooking oil, then the greens—if using more than one type, either start the tougher-seeming ones first and add the more tender later or cook them separately. Add salt. When the greens begin to wilt, turn them around with tongs, getting the top leaves to the bottom, and continue to cook, adding splashes of water if it sounds sizzly. Taste a leaf and a stem for both tenderness and seasoning. Keep cooking if needed, add-ing salt, oil, or water as required. When the greens are tender, move them to the perimeter, put the garlic center-skillet, and add a little oil if it's dry there. When the garlic smells just right, a bare minute, bring in the greens and stir them around. Set the greens aside on a tilted plate to let the liquid run out as they cool. Discard the excess liquid. Chop the greens finely and put them in a medium bowl with the ricotta, ¼ cup grated pecorino, the olive oil, and lemon juice or vinegar. Mix well, taste, and adjust.

Start rolling out your pasta on a pasta machine, making it incrementally thin-ner until it is just translucent, about the thickness of heavy paper or cardstock. On my machine, this is number 6. Because pasta dough doesn't always behave the same way, I sometimes roll the dough through 6 twice if I want it thinner, but not so thin as number 7. On a floured surface, cut the long sheet of pasta into shorter lengths of about 16 inches. Keep one to work with first, sprinkle the rest with flour, stack them, and set them aside, covered so that they don't dry out.

Brush any loose flour off the sheet you're starting with and lightly brush or spritz it with water so it will seal when folded. Place 3 rounded tablespoon-fuls of filling along the center of the sheet, one in the very middle with the others on either side, halfway between the center and the edge. Fold the pasta toward you and over the filling and, starting at one end so that the air can escape from the other, smooth the dough around the lumps of filling. Your fingers should slide over the pasta as you go—if the pasta is grabbing and wrinkling, dip your fingers in flour before you curve them around each filling bump. Once sealed, use a sharp knife or fluted pasta cutter to cut the pansotti into big squares or curved into half-moons. (Save 4 or 5 scraps of the doubled pasta to boil with the pansotti—you'll taste them to determine doneness.) Repeat to use up all of the filling and set the finished pansotti on floured trays, making sure that they do not touch one another or they will stick. Refrigerate them if you're not cooking soon.

Bring a big pot of water to a boil and add salt. Have a skillet ready that will hold the pansotti. Slip the pansotti and pasta scraps into the boiling water, lowering the heat so it continues to boil, but more gently. Taste one of the scraps after 5 minutes to check for doneness, and when it's close, ladle about ¼ cup water into the skillet and keep it on low heat with 2 tablespoons olive oil. When the pansotti are done, dip them out of the pot and into the waiting skillet, swirl to coat, and place them on a warm platter with splashes of the oily water. Spoon half of the salsa di noci over and pass the rest at the table along with cheese for grating.

Winter

CITRUS SALAD WITH GINGER, CILANTRO, AND SAFFRON-TOASTED PISTACHIOS

When winter arrives, we are especially eager to keep the chill gray at bay and cook dishes as full of color as they are flavorful. A naturally sunny direction to turn is toward the bins of citrus fruits that arrive at the markets in amazing diversity. Sweetened by the cold, citrus fruits need only careful peeling and slicing to make them both elegant and easy to enjoy, and a savory element or two added to sensibly move them from breakfast table to dinner table.

Makes 6 servings

1 to 2 teaspoons grated ginger (about 1 inch)

1 batch citrus zest vinaigrette (page 245)

1 small red onion

Salt

2 tablespoons red wine vinegar

4 to 6 oranges (about 2½ pounds), Valencia or navel, blood or Cara Cara . . . or Ruby or Oro Blanco grapefruits . . . or Satsuma, Pixie, or Page tangerines . . . or a rainbow of several

Leaves from 8 cilantro sprigs

Scant ¼ cup pistachios toasted with saffron and lemon (see page 9)

A handful of salad greens such as frisée, or small mizuna, or water- or peppercress, washed and dried

Freshly ground black pepper

Stir the ginger into the citrus vinaigrette and set aside.

Peel the onion and cut some thin slices and pop apart the rings. A whole onion's worth of rings is probably too much, so save the rest for another use. Put the onion rings in a medium bowl and add ¼ teaspoon salt, the vinegar, and cold water to just cover. Add a few ice cubes and let the onion rings temper and crisp up while you prepare the oranges.

With a sharp, narrow-bladed knife, cut slices from the top and bottom of an orange, as if you were lopping off the polar ice caps. Cut off enough so that you see a small circle of the flesh within. Set the orange on one of the flat ends and, in a motion that describes a curve, carve off a strip of skin just down to the flesh. Rotate the orange and repeat taking off strips until it is skinless. Trim off any pithy bits you may have missed. If the membranes and core of the orange are tender enough—cut a slice to taste and see—you can slice the orange crosswise into rounds. Otherwise, holding the peeled orange in your palm, cut the segments out from between the membranes, making clean little wedges. You may want an extra orange if you're cutting segments—the yield is a little lower. Repeat with the remaining oranges.

Arrange the oranges on a platter, sprinkle them lightly with salt, and top them with the drained onion rings. Spoon most of the vinaigrette over the oranges and onion, and sprinkle the cilantro leaves and pistachios around. Dress the frisée or other salad greens with the remaining vinaigrette and a little salt and black pepper and use them to garnish the platter—scattered all over or piled in the center.

FISH WITH CRISP SKIN, CELERY ROOT PUREE, AND CELERY AND LEMON SALSA

Pan-frying skin-on fish in the al mattone style—weighted for crisp skin—is ideal for cooking very fresh fillets of wild king salmon, black cod, or white sea bass. With summer tomatoes and herbs, it can be a showstopper, but it may be even more impressive in winter, when it can both comfort and surprise, especially served with a spoonful of warm satiny puree and a lemony celery salsa for brightness. Thin fillets won't work for this method, as they cook through before the skin has a chance to get crisp—the fillets should be at least 1½ inches thick. To weight them, use a foil-wrapped, heavy skillet that's a bit smaller than the one you're frying in.

Makes 6 servings

1 to 1½ pounds celery root

Salt

1 pint half-and-half

1 tablespoon butter

Six 3-ounce portions skin-on fish (see ideas above)

Freshly ground black pepper

1 cup thinly sliced celery

Juice and zest of ½ lemon

1 tablespoon chopped parsley

3 tablespoons good olive oil

2 tablespoons cooking oil, olive or vegetable

Peel the celery root, split it in half, and cut the halves into slices about ½ inch thick. Rinse and put them in a saucepan with ¾ teaspoon salt and just enough of the half-and-half to barely cover (save any extra for another use). Bring the liquid to a simmer, stirring occasionally to be sure there's nothing sticking, and cook the celery root until it is very tender, about 20 minutes—taste to be sure: it should be nearly falling apart. Lift the celery root out of the saucepan and into a blender or food processor, add the butter, and puree until very smooth, adding just enough of the cooking liquid to make it go. Taste, adjust, and set aside. Reserve the remaining cooking liquid to use for reheating.

Season the fish with black pepper and ½ teaspoon salt and set aside.

Bring a small pot of water to a boil and add salt and then the sliced celery. Cook until it is tender but still crunchy, about 4 minutes. Dip the slices out onto a plate to cool. In a small bowl, mix the cooled celery with the lemon juice and zest, ¼ teaspoon salt, black pepper, parsley, and the olive oil. Stir, taste, adjust, and set aside.

Reheat the celery root puree in a double boiler or skillet, stirring to prevent scorching and, if needed, adding some of the half-and-half it was cooked in to smooth it out.

Meanwhile, heat a skillet to high; add the cooking oil and, right away, the fish portions with the skin side down. Lower the heat to medium-high and place a weight on top of the fish. Cook until the skin is quite browned and the flesh is nearly cooked, 5 to 7 minutes, depending on thickness, then turn the fillets over to finish cooking, but *do not* re-cover them or you'll lose the crispness of the skin.

While the fish finishes (peek in on the nonskin side to make sure they are just cooked through), put a shallow dollop of celery root puree in the middle of six warmed plates, or spread it thickly on a platter. Set the pieces of fish atop the puree and spoon the salsa around. Marvel.

JERUSALEM ARTICHOKE SALAD, WHICH IS GOOD WITH PARMESAN AND VERY GOOD WITH BLACK TRUFFLE

Jerusalem artichokes are in fact sunflower tubers and as such taste, when sliced raw, both of cold earth and warm sun. The parsley leaves play their part to practically make this salad a science project, a diorama of ground, growth, and photosynthesis. And Parmesan.

Makes 6 servings

1 small garlic clove, pounded with a pinch of salt

2 teaspoons lemon juice

1 teaspoon champagne vinegar or white wine vinegar

3 tablespoons good olive oil

Scant pound Jerusalem artichokes, peeled or scrubbed (unless their skins are very thin and fresh-looking), submerged in cold water

Salt

3 tablespoons chopped parsley

Parmesan

In a small bowl, mix the garlic paste, lemon juice, and vinegar and let sit for a few minutes. Stir in the oil and set the dressing aside.

Slice the Jerusalem artichokes as thinly as you can, carefully using a mandoline or your very sharpest knife—in either case, with your keenest attention. Toss in a medium bowl with ¼ teaspoon salt, the parsley, and most of the vinaigrette. Taste, adjust, and spread out flat on a platter. Sprinkle the remaining vinaigrette over and make shavings of Parmesan with a vegetable peeler to scatter around.

* *To add black truffle, crush or grate some in a separate bowl, mix it with olive oil and a pinch of salt, cover it, and let it sit somewhere warm for 20 minutes. Spoon the truffle oil over the salad instead of the last of the vinaigrette.*
* *Shave fennel or mushrooms—very fresh, firm porcini are nice—to toss with the Jerusalem artichokes.*
* *Add some pounded anchovy fillets to the vinaigrette and sprinkle the salad with chopped hard-boiled egg.*

BELGIAN ENDIVE AND SMOKED COD SALAD WITH BEETS AND WALNUT VINAIGRETTE

My dad gave me a stovetop smoker a few years ago, and I like to use it for smoking duck breasts, pork tenderloins, and fish. It's a hot smoker with a simple design, easy to use and clean, and not too expensive either. Order one at Cameronsproducts.com, or just order the fine wood chips—I like alderwood—and rig up your own smoker: Lay a square of aluminum foil flat on the bottom of a kettle or wide pot. Put a spoonful of wood chips on the foil, make 3 little foil balls to set around the wood chips, and balance a lightly oiled baking dish, like a cake pan or pie tin, on the foil balls. Put whatever you're going to smoke in the baking dish, put the whole contraption on a burner, cover the kettle, and start smoking over medium-low heat. Unlike cold smoking, hot smoking fully cooks the food, so check for doneness in the usual way: cut in and take a peek.

Makes 6 servings

1 bunch red beets

Salt

2 teaspoons red wine vinegar

Good olive oil

12 ounces fish fillet—black cod, ling cod, or other flaky but not super-delicate fish

1 teaspoon brown sugar

Leaves from 6 thyme sprigs

3 Belgian endive heads—white, red, or a combination

1 tablespoon chopped chives

2 tablespoons chopped chervil or 1 teaspoon chopped tarragon

⅓ cup toasted and chopped walnuts (see page 9)

1 batch walnut vinaigrette (page 244)

Freshly ground black pepper

Cut the greens off the beets and save them, if they're in good shape, for another use (page 23). Rinse the beets thoroughly and boil them in well-salted water or, even better, roast them (see the instructions on page 62). Using your hands, slip the skins off the cooled beets and cut them into quarters. Puree them in a food processor, blender, or food mill and mix in the red wine vinegar, ¼ cup oil, and ¼ teaspoon salt. Taste, adjust, and set aside.

Meanwhile, season the fish with ¾ teaspoon salt and the brown sugar and leave at room temperature for 20 minutes to let the seasoning soak in. Pat the fish dry with paper towels and sprinkle it with the thyme leaves, pressing them on with your fingers. Smoke the fish (see introduction) and set it aside to cool.

Separate the Belgian endive leaves by cutting a small slice off the bottom, then pulling off the leaves that are released. Continue cutting and pulling leaves until they are all loose. Put them in a mixing bowl with the chopped herbs and walnuts and dress with most of the vinaigrette and a sprinkle of salt and pepper. Taste and adjust. Spread the beet puree on a large serving platter, using the back of a spoon to swirl it out nearly to the edges, and arrange the Belgian endive leaves on top. Break the smoked fish into pieces and sprinkle it over the salad. Spoon the remaining vinaigrette over and serve.

RADICCHIO SALAD WITH HERBS, SUN-DRIED TOMATOES, AND CRÈME FRAÎCHE DRESSING

Chioggia radicchio, the commonest red and white type, is great for this salad. If your market also offers speckled Castelfranco, pale Pan di Zucchero, curling crimson Tardivo fingers, or other exotic types, they can add great color and texture variation. A small head of escarole or frisée, or a handful of arugula mixed in wouldn't be wrong. The crème fraîche tempers the bitterness of the radicchio, and the sun-dried tomatoes get together with the herbs to remind you that summer is not that far off.

Makes 6 servings

1 small shallot, finely diced

½ garlic clove, pounded with ¼ teaspoon salt

1 teaspoon lemon juice

1 teaspoon red or white wine vinegar

Freshly ground black pepper

3 tablespoons crème fraîche (page 248)

2 medium radicchio heads (about 1½ pounds), cored, leaves separated, washed, and spun dry

1 tablespoon chopped parsley

2 tablespoons roughly chopped mint

1 tablespoon chopped chives

1 teaspoon chopped marjoram

¼ cup chopped sun-dried tomatoes, soaked in hot water for 45 minutes before chopping if using dried, or drained if using oil-packed

¼ teaspoon salt

1 tablespoon good olive oil

In a small bowl, combine the shallot, garlic paste, lemon juice, vinegar, and black pepper. Let the mixture marinate for a few minutes, stir in the crème fraîche, and set aside.

In a salad bowl, toss the radicchio with the herbs, sun-dried tomatoes, salt, oil, and most of the dressing. Use your hands to mix well and coat all the leaves, taste, adjust, and stripe with the remaining dressing.

* *Grate bottarga di muggine (salted and pressed mullet roe) over the salad.*

AND THEN:
SECOND COURSES

Chez Panisse is closed on Sundays to restore sanity and order to building and staff alike: a day for maintenance and some deep cleaning. It's also one of my favorite times to be there, a rare moment of quiet when I can see the place through a less kaleidoscopic lens. The stillness of the kitchen seems to amplify the smells of cold ashes in the hearth, a lingering fatty savor of Saturday night's roast, faded red wine, and, in the dining room, flowers and snuffed candles. Upstairs, the floors are getting a polish—a week's worth of heels and scuffs to be buffed out. I smile my weekly smile at Chime, who does the polishing, as I go up to the bar to make a coffee. The aroma of the grinder and the steamer's hiss are, without a crowd to muffle them, more pointed here, too. The happy weekend crush long gone, the rooms look good empty, showing more of the windows, wood, copper, and Pagnol movie posters. It feels calm but potent, dining rooms waiting to be filled, anticipating the busy week to come.

In the walk-in, it's different, like a sort of archaeological debriefing, the events of the previous night spelled out in leftovers. Here are the three asparagus soufflé puddings we made for a table of vegetarians who never showed up, here the extra cup of herb salsa that I insisted we'd need and clearly hadn't, and there the dairy-free soup made for a vegan who, it turned out, was unaccountably fine with cream and butter. If the night was especially busy, there might be some empty containers left unbussed, some salad plates that no longer need chilling, maybe a bucket full of what was ice for chilling champagne and, hey, half a bottle of champagne. In terms of messes, it's a tiny one, entirely manageable, the sort that includes a couple of fading slices of prosciutto and the last three hazelnut truffles.

Quiet Sunday is for salting fish, making confit, and checking on the meats to be served that week, often whole animals to cut and trim, season and marinate, and tie into roasts. The farms we buy from are the best, and their birds and beasts are reliably delicious. They are also justifiably expensive and we gladly pay the price, use every bit, eat considered portions, and allow the other best farmers' herbs and vegetables to do the rest.

When there is an extra portion or two of fish, the last couple of quail, or the end of a lamb loin, Sunday can also provide the meat of a chef's dinner at home, and an opportunity for trying out a new technique or a sauce and for taking care of that half bottle of champagne.

VEGETABLE COUSCOUS WITH TWO SAUCES

This is one of those undogmatically vegetarian dishes that, though meatless, attracts even the snarliest carnivores. Unsurprisingly, the humble chickpea, chubby yet muscular, pale yet potent and ready to deliver flavor, texture, and meaty protein, is once again our salvation. My favorite legume provides broth as well, the flavorful bean cooking liquid rendering meat stock unneeded. Sturdy, stewy stage established, you can bring the best vegetables of the season to star, and any season will do: artichokes, little turnips, and peas in spring; peppers, green beans, and tomatoes in summer; cauliflower, kale, and squash in fall; or carrots, sunchokes, and rutabagas in winter. All this, plus two sauces, and vegetarian seems less limitation and more celebration.

Though granular, couscous is not a grain. It is made from wheat flour, like pasta in little pellets. Unlike pasta, however, couscous is not exactly quick and easy to cook. Do not be deterred, but the truth is that couscous is kind of a pain to make right, and I am not even talking about rolling the grains by hand, which is more of a pain and, in my humble opinion, not really worth it (with apologies to Moroccan grandmas and Paula Wolfert). Just steaming the store-bought stuff properly takes stamina—in order for it to be as tender and fluffy as you want it to be, it must be dampened, cooked, dampened, cooked, dampened, and cooked . . . and sometimes dampened and cooked once more. Thankfully, there are but three ingredients—couscous, salt, water—and the technique is easy enough. You just have to keep doing it and doing it while you get the rest of the meal together. It's not so hard, the airy texture is worth the trouble, and, happily, cooked couscous keeps well, so make extra and your effort will keep on giving.

At home, I have a pot and colander that match up well for steaming couscous—I twist up a dampened kitchen towel to serve as a gasket between the two, preventing steam from escaping out the sides and sending it up where couscous awaits cooking. At the restaurant we have a two-tiered affair, a couscoussier, made just for this.

1 large yellow onion

2 cups dried chickpeas, soaked overnight in cold water to cover by 3 inches

2 garlic cloves, skins left on, and cracked

Cilantro and/or parsley stems

1 bay leaf

1 small carrot

1 celery stalk

½ small tomato

Salt

2 cups dried couscous

2 tablespoons good olive oil or melted unsalted butter

¼ cup cooking oil, olive or vegetable

2 teaspoons cumin seeds, toasted and ground (see page 9)

1 teaspoon coriander seeds, toasted and ground

1 teaspoon fennel seeds, toasted and ground

½ teaspoon caraway seeds, toasted and ground

1 teaspoon paprika

Greens and vegetables in season

Chermoula sauce (page 259)

Harissa sauce (page 261)

Dice the onion. Set the dice aside and add the onion butts to a medium sauce-pan with the drained chickpeas, garlic, herb stems, bay, carrot, celery, tomato, and ½ teaspoon salt. Add water to cover by 3 inches and bring the pot to a boil over high heat. Reduce to a quiet bubble, skim off any foam that has risen, and taste the water. If it doesn't seem pleasantly, potably saline, add a bit more salt. Cook until the chickpeas are very tender, about 2 hours. Their inner texture should be creamy—keep cooking if they seem at all chalky. When done, pluck out the aromatics and let the chickpeas be in their precious liquid: it will be the broth that couscous calls for.

Get the couscous steaming while the chickpeas cook. If you can rig it up, it's nice to steam the couscous over the simmering chickpeas, capturing their fla-vorful steam. Or, you can just steam over plain water. Put the couscous in a mixing bowl, cover it with cold water, and drain immediately. Leave it for 15 minutes while you get your steamer situation set and steamy, then use your hands to break up the now-clumpy couscous, rubbing it between your palms to separate the grains. Sprinkle it with ½ teaspoon salt, mix, and pour it into your steamer. Make sure no steam is escaping around the sides; it should all, or very nearly all, be passing up through the couscous—I use a damp rolled-up kitchen towel to chink the gaps around. Cover and steam for 15 minutes. Remove the couscous from the heat, sprinkle it with ¼ cup water, stir, and let it absorb for 15 minutes. Repeat the steam and sprinkle twice more. The couscous should look lighter in color and feel very tender and fluffy in the mouth. If not, sprinkle and steam again. When it's done, turn off the heat, drizzle with the olive oil, stir to coat, and leave the couscous in the steamer to reheat when it's time.

Meanwhile, heat a skillet to high and add the cooking oil and then the diced onion, ½ teaspoon salt, and the spices. Stir until things get going, then lower the heat to medium and cook, stirring occasionally, until the onion is very soft but not browned, about 20 minutes. Add a splash of water from time to time if needed to fully cook with minimum browning. Stir the onion into the chickpeas, rinsing the pan with a little of their cooking liquid to get all the flavor.

Sauces made, couscous steamed, and chickpea base ready to go, you can now cook your vegetables. Sauté some greens with garlic to mix into the chickpeas while you roast cauliflower and slices of squash, say. Or sauté red and yellow peppers to mix in while boiling green beans to dress with oil and salt and strew over a bowl of the chickpea mixture. Possibilities abound—go with what's best at the market. Just make sure everything is well cooked (it is a stew, after all, and the parts shouldn't really be crunchy) and that the chickpeas have plenty of liquid, then spoon them over the couscous and pass bowls of chermoula and harissa.

NOT-POTLUCK LASAGNA OR 15-LAYER LASAGNA

If you have ever shuddered at an unfortunate potluck buffet as the viscera of a lurid lasagna cools and seizes in flimsy foil next to wilted supermarket salads, have I got a pasta revelation for you! Lasagna done this way is slim and elegant, where that other is two kinds of thick, maybe three. Layered and light, with a texture almost crepe-like, there is still enough savory melt to comfort. Try this lasagna of many layers and find, as I did, that it offers full recovery from the dispiriting effects of bad buffet.

Makes 6 generous servings

Cooking oil, olive or vegetable

¾ pound spinach, stemmed, washed, and drip-dried, not spun

Salt

2 garlic cloves, finely chopped

12 ounces ricotta

½ cup cream

½ cup grated Parmesan

3 cups warm béchamel (page 254)

2½ cups summer marinara sauce (page 267)

10 ounces mozzarella, grated

1 batch egg pasta dough (recipe follows)

Heat a skillet to medium-high and add 1 tablespoon oil, then the spinach and ¼ teaspoon salt. Stirring occasionally, cook until wilted and tender, 3 to 4 minutes. If there is a lot of water in the skillet, tip it off and move the spinach to the edges. Add a bit more oil and the garlic, stir it a little as it cooks and smells good but don't let it brown. Bring in the spinach and mix it all up. Set the greens aside on a tilted plate to allow the liquid to run out as they cool. Discard the excess liquid, chop the spinach finely, and mix it in a medium bowl with the ricotta, cream, and ½ teaspoon salt.

Stir the Parmesan into the béchamel and you have your fillings ready: tomato sauce, mozzarella, spinach and ricotta, and béchamel sauce. There will be 4 filling layers of tomato sauce and mozzarella and 3 of spinach and ricotta, so apportion them that way—you don't have to divide them into every bowl in the house, just visually get a sense of fourths and thirds. Brush a 3-quart lasagna-shaped baking dish with oil.

Bring a large pot of water to a boil and add plenty of salt—the pasta will be rolled thin and will cook in less than a minute, so the water should taste not of the sea quite, but definitely salted. Have ready a bowl of ice water to cool the pasta in once boiled and a couple of clean kitchen towels to blot it dry. Using a pasta maker, roll the pasta incrementally thinner and thinner, until it is nearly translucent (through number 6 twice on my Atlas), and cut it into sheets just shy of the length of the baking dish you are using—they will grow slightly in cooking. Save any scraps to fill in gaps. Drop 2 sheets of pasta into the boiling water and nudge them around with a spider so they don't stick to each other. Boil for 30 to 45 seconds and when the pasta is tender but still has plenty of bite, dip them out and put them into the ice water. Keep the water at a boil for cooking the next sheets. Let the pasta cool for half a minute, then lift it out and blot dry on the kitchen towels.

Lay one of the sheets in the dish, trimming if needed to make it fit flat. Spoon over a fourth of the tomato sauce, and sprinkle on a fourth of the grated mozzarella. The amount of filling on each layer may seem meager, but maintain restraint—the many layers will add up to just the right amount. Streak lightly with béchamel, about ⅓ cup—if it has gotten very thick, you may need to carefully warm it up, or thin it with a little milk. Lay the other cooked sheet on top, spread it with a third of the ricotta mixture, and again streak with béchamel. Repeat until you've assembled 4 layers of tomato filling, 3 of ricotta, and 8 of pasta, rolling and boiling more sheets as you go. Every layer gets béchamel except the top one: brush it with oil.

At this point, you can set the lasagna aside to bake later: keep it at room temperature or refrigerate it for a few hours or overnight, and then bring it back to room temperature before baking. Heat the oven to 425°F and bake uncovered, until the lasagna is bubbly, browned, and hot in the center—slip the blade of a paring knife into the middle, hold it there for 5 seconds, withdraw the blade, and feel it to be sure the center is piping hot. If it needs a little more time and you're worried about too much browning or drying out, cover the dish with foil and bake a bit more. If the whole lasagna puffs up like a pillow, poke it to release the steam buildup.

* *When tomatoes are out of season, replace the marinara sauce with 1½ pounds of mushrooms, wild or cultivated, sliced, sautéed with garlic and thyme, and chopped. Stir a little cream in with the mushrooms if you have it. Double the amount of spinach and delete the ricotta.*
* *Go all green: make the spinach pasta version of the egg pasta and cook lots more greens: a little sorrel in with the spinach, some nettles or chard, whatever looks good. Use more ricotta, too, a whole pound, and instead of mixing it with the greens, mix cream with them, put little dots of seasoned ricotta on top, and stripe with plenty of béchamel.*

Egg Pasta

This recipe makes enough pasta for agnolotti, ravioli, or lasagna to serve 6. Double it if it's for hand-cut pasta like fettuccine.

1 cup all-purpose flour	2 eggs
¾ cup semolina flour	2 egg yolks
⅛ teaspoon salt	2 teaspoons olive oil

Measure the flours into a large mixing bowl. Add the salt. In a separate bowl, whisk the eggs, yolks, and oil until completely mixed. Using a wooden spoon or your fingers, slowly stir the egg mixture into the flour. Use your hands to keep mixing the dough until it just holds together. It's okay if it's a little crumbly; it will come together as the flour continues to absorb moisture. If it's just too dry, add another egg yolk or a little water, but you don't want it to be sticky at all. Divide the dough into 2 or 3 lumps, shape them into balls, and then flatten

them into discs. Set the discs on a plate, cover them with plastic and a kitchen towel, and leave them alone at room temperature for 1 hour or up to 4 hours.

Crank one of the discs of dough through the widest setting on your pasta machine. You may need to flatten it a bit with your hands or a rolling pin to get it started. Once through, if it seems sticky, sprinkle a little flour onto it, fold it over, and roll it through again at the same setting. Keep folding and rolling until the dough becomes very even, smooth, and, ideally, neatly rectangular— six passes or so. Roll the rectangle up, tuck it back under the towel, repeat with the rest, and let them all sit for half an hour.

If you are making lasagna or stuffed pasta, roll the dough out as you go. If you are making hand-cut pasta, see double-zero pasta (page 78) for instructions on how to cut them.

* *To make spinach pasta, replace one of the whole eggs with a small handful of raw, washed, and spun-dry spinach leaves. Put the egg, yolks, oil, and spinach in a blender, puree until the mixture is smooth, and proceed with the recipe.*

FISH FILLETS STUFFED WITH BREAD CRUMBS, SAFFRON, PINE NUTS, AND CURRANTS

I wouldn't say it to a Sicilian, but pine nuts and currants go together like peanut butter and jelly. In this recipe there are even bread crumbs to complete the sandwichy-ness, though fish, even if nestled in the Wonder, probably wouldn't make most kids' lunch box cut. Swordfish is traditional in this dish, but it's problematic for several reasons I won't go into (but you can easily look up), so I use sole. Squid are wonderful stuffed and baked like this, too, as are whole gutted sardines if you're okay with little bones, or sardine fillets if you're not.

Makes 6 servings

3 tablespoons olive oil

1 small yellow onion, diced

Salt

½ teaspoon saffron

1 teaspoon fennel seeds, toasted and ground (see page 9)

1 garlic clove, chopped

Crushed red pepper flakes

¾ cup toasted bread crumbs (page 79)

1½ tablespoons toasted pine nuts or almonds, coarsely chopped (see page 9)

1½ tablespoons currants or raisins, plumped in hot water for 20 minutes and drained and, if using raisins, coarsely chopped

1 teaspoon chopped marjoram or oregano

2 tablespoons chopped parsley

2 tablespoons good olive oil

6 medium sole fillets (about 1½ pounds), split lengthwise and the few bones from near the collar cut out

Freshly ground black pepper

¼ cup white wine or water

Heat a skillet to high and add the olive oil, then the onion and salt. Stir until it gets going, then lower the heat and add the saffron and fennel seeds. Cook over low heat, adding a splash of water from time to time if needed, until the

onion is soft but not browned, about 15 minutes. Move the onion to make a bare spot in the center of the skillet, add the garlic and red pepper flakes, and cook until the garlic smells good, but don't let it brown. Bring in the onion, stir, and turn out into a medium bowl to cool. Put the bread crumbs, pine nuts, currants, herbs, and good olive oil into the bowl with the onion. Stir well, taste, and adjust.

Heat the oven to 450°F.

Lay the fillets out and season both sides with salt and pepper. Visually divide the stuffing into 12 parts, one for each fillet. Place a portion of stuffing atop each fillet and either roll it up, or simply fold it over, tucking in stray bits of stuffing as you go and laying the finished pieces in a baking dish. Brush or pat the top surfaces of the fish with oil, pour the wine into the dish, and bake until just cooked through, 8 to 12 minutes, depending on thickness. Rolled fillets generally take longer than folded. Peek at the center to be sure the fish is no longer translucent. Serve right away or later at room temperature.

* *Serve as a first course with tomato vinaigrette (page 242).*

* *Make a Sicilo-Franco-fusion as a hot first course with beurre blanc (page 247) and mint.*

* *Serve as dinner with vinaigrette or butter sauce and a vegetable like asparagus, green beans, cauliflower, or sautéed greens.*

* *Instead of fish, stuff scooped-out summer squashes or eggplants, or sections of them, roasted with salt and oil until just tender. Spoon the stuffing into the cavities and roast again until browned on top, about 10 minutes more. Nice with either of the sauces mentioned above or with a splash of whichever vinaigrette is dressing the salad sitting next to them for lunch.*

FISH AND SHELLFISH SOUP FOR SUMMER

I have never had the bouillabaisse my friend Jérôme makes when he is in his native South of France, but the versions he makes here in California are the best I've ever eaten. In summer he uses plenty of ripe red tomatoes, and he always likes to cook the soup over a wood fire with a lid propped just so, boosting flavor with the resulting smoky vortex. Once, it is said, he even slipped into the pot a still-smoldering coal, stirring and skimming as it hissed like a lump of lava sinking through a steaming saffron sea.

Making a soup like this is involved and does take some time (and it's a little messy; you'll want to formulate a plan for what to do with the squidly bits and the fish bones after you've strained the stock. I bag and freeze them to put out with the trash, or compost, on collection day). Completely worth it, and though the saffron is both essential and expensive, the other ingredients are fairly humble—fish bones are hopefully available at your fishmonger and are often given for free, or are at least very cheap. The seafoods must be very fresh, of course, but needn't be fancy—cheaper varieties like rockfishes and squid are best for flavorful fish soups. Inexpensive clams are happy to sub for pricy wild-caught shrimp (farmed shrimp are less delicious, very problematic, and not recommended—you can easily look up why).

The broth really is best eaten the same day, so making it very far ahead is not an option, unless you freeze it. You can, and should, cook the aromatic vegetables, trim and season the fish, and make the broth earlier in the day. Refrigerate them all and then go rub lemons on your arms like Susan Sarandon, put on your party dress, put on some music, and put the whole thing together in effortless (!) style when it's time.

1 pound fish fillets (meaty, flaky fish like rockfish, snapper, halibut, sea bass)

12 to 18 wild-caught shrimp, depending on size, or the same number of small clams

1 pound squid

1 fennel bulb

1 leek

2 large ripe red tomatoes

Cooking oil, olive or vegetable

1 heaping teaspoon fennel seeds

1 heaping teaspoon coriander seeds

1½ teaspoons saffron threads

2 bay leaves

3 (½-inch-wide) strips orange peel

1 dried mild chili, seeds removed (New Mexico, Hatch, or sweet paprika)

2 pounds whitefish bones, cut into chunks, rinsed and any bloody bits removed

1 small yellow onion, roughly sliced

2 celery stalks, roughly sliced

6 thyme sprigs

6 parsley sprigs, plus additional chopped leaves for serving

4 garlic cloves, skins left on, cracked

¾ cup white wine

Salt

Freshly ground black pepper

Fresh or toasted bread, for serving

1 cup aïoli (page 265)

First thing is to trim the fish fillets—cut away any bony parts or scrappy-looking bits and save them to add to the bones for the broth. Cut the fillets into 8 roughly even pieces and refrigerate. Peel the shrimp, saving and refrigerating all the shells, devein them, and refrigerate. If the squid are whole, they need cleaning. Cut off the tentacles just above the eyes and pop out the hard beak at their center. Set the tentacle aside and, sliding not slicing with your chef's knife, squeegee the guts from the squid bodies, making sure to get them all and especially the quill that looks like a piece of thin, clear plastic but is actually skeletal. Tidy the ink and squish from your cutting board, slice the squid bodies into ½-inch rings, and refrigerate the rings and tentacles.

To make the broth, trim the green tops from the fennel and the leek. You want a loose cup of each of the trimmings—the remaining parts will be used later. Wash and drain the trimmings and set them aside. Cut one of the tomatoes into chunks and set aside.

Heat a stockpot to medium. Add ¼ cup oil, the fennel and coriander seeds, 1 teaspoon of the saffron, the bay leaves, orange peel, and chili and stir occasionally for 1 minute. Add the reserved shrimp shells and cook for a minute more. Now add the fish bones, raise the heat to high, and stir occasionally for a few minutes. Add the onion, celery, tomato chunks, fennel and leek trimmings, thyme, parsley, and garlic. Stir for a couple minutes more, then add 2 quarts of cold water and bring to a simmer. Do not allow the stock to boil hard— you want a shimmery murmur, not a rollicking bubble. Stir once to make sure nothing is sticking to the bottom. Skim off any foam that appears, add the wine, and simmer gently for 30 minutes, continuing to skim foam as it rises to the surface. Turn off the heat and let the stock sit for 30 minutes, then strain. After the strained stock settles for 5 minutes, skim it again. Stir in ½ teaspoon salt, taste, and add a little more if needed. Refrigerate the stock unless you are using it now.

Dice the reserved fennel bulb and leek. Wash well and drain. Grind the remaining ½ teaspoon saffron to powder. Peel, seed, and dice the remaining tomato, or just dice it if you prefer.

Heat a skillet or Dutch oven large enough to hold the fish, shellfish, and broth to high. Add ¼ cup oil, the diced fennel and leek, the ground saffron, and salt and stir until things get going, then turn the heat to medium-low and continue cooking, stirring occasionally, until tender, about 10 minutes. Add the diced tomato and a bit more salt, raise the heat, and cook for a minute or two, then add the fish broth. Season the fish, shrimp, and squid with salt and pepper while you bring the soup to a simmer. Slip the fishes into the soup and simmer until they are cooked, about 5 minutes. Ladle into warm bowls, sprinkle with

parsley, and serve with fresh or toasted bread. Pass a bowl of aïoli for dolloping, and cold rosé or white wine for fun.

* *Use different varieties of fish and shellfish if they seem best at the market. Salmon bones are not the best for stock-making, but chunks of wild-caught salmon fillets or steaks would be appropriately summery to cook in it. Clams, mussels, crab, lobster . . . all good.*
* *Skip the diced tomatoes and instead set a slow-baked tomato in each bowl of soup, for drama and interactivity—soup eaters crush and stir in the tomato as they spoon along.*
* *Pass a bowl of romesco sauce (page 252) instead of aïoli.*

FISH SOUP IN WINTER

The first time I made a soup like this, it was a disaster. I was working at the wonderful, eccentric Biba restaurant in Boston, under the leadership of Lydia Shire in a kitchen that was inspired, impossible, and never boring. The menu changed seasonally, and one of my new dishes was littleneck clam and sorrel soup. New-menu day was always a three-ring event, with juggling cooks and sous-chefs jumping through flaming hoops while explaining ingredients and techniques as the first orders barreled in. My instructions were: steam open the clams with wine and broth, quickly tip the hot liquid into the blender, add a handful of sorrel leaves, spin to a steaming emerald froth, pour the froth over the clams, and send it quickly to the table before the color faded. But the steam and froth were too much for the blender, blowing its top with a pop and spraying impatient waiters, frantic cooks, and the now-silent room with hot green foam. "Bursting with flavor," I wish I had said—though I didn't—as I avoided Lydia's glare, licked my lips (it *was* good), wiped the walls, and started another order.

To make this soup, use the Fish Soup for Summer recipe, but leave out the diced tomato from the leek-fennel mixture and omit the tomato, orange peel, and chili from the broth. Just before serving, push a handful of raw sorrel leaves down into your blender and pour a couple of ladlefuls of broth over the sorrel (it's okay if some of the leeks and fennel get in there, but not okay if fishes do), hold the lid on with a kitchen towel, pulse the blender very briefly a couple of times to release the steam, and then let it rip to spin up all bright green. Stir this lemony liquor back into the pot and serve the soup on the double with crusty bread or toasts and passed bowls of aïoli.

PAN-FRIED FISHCAKES

One Wednesday morning some years ago at Chez Panisse, my former co-chef Leah found herself with a quantity of braised beef, beautiful stuff, left over from a slow Tuesday night. Braised meats being one of those things that only get better the next day, it was never in doubt that it was going on the menu, but Leah was looking for something other than the usual ragù and pasta that we all adored.

"What if I shred it," she asked me, "mix it with a little mirepoix, bread crumbs, herbs, and egg to bind it, and we'll make it into little patties to pan-fry, breaded, crispy . . . with beets and horseradish crème fraîche!?"

"Sounds like the best lunch ever," I said.

Later, when she was proofing the menu copy before service, I saw over her shoulder that she had them listed as beefcakes.

"Good one," I said, smiling at the joke. "What are you really going to call them?"

She looked at me. It wasn't a joke.

"You can't write beefcakes on the menu."

"Why? We do fishcakes," she said, annoyed and a little defensive. "We can't make beefcakes?"

"We can make them, but you know what beefcake is, right?"

She didn't. I explained.

"Oh!" she said. "Oh."

She changed the wording.

Fishcakes, like cakes of beef, would be nice served with a salad of beets and some horseradish or herb crème fraîche (page 249). Or with slaw (page 230) and a spoonful of aïoli (page 265) or other mayonnaise. Green beans and tomato vinaigrette (page 242)?

Cooking oil, olive or vegetable

1 yellow onion, diced

1 carrot, finely diced

1 celery stalk, finely diced

Salt

1 lime

1 pound cod fillet, or other mild
white fish

Freshly ground black pepper

⅓ cup heavy cream

¼ cup chopped cilantro leaves and
stems

1 jalapeño, seeded and finely diced
(or less or more)

3½ cups fresh bread crumbs

4 eggs

1 cup all-purpose flour

Heat a skillet to high and add ¼ cup cooking oil, then the onion, carrot, celery, and ½ teaspoon salt. Stir until it gets going, then turn to medium and cook, stirring occasionally, until the vegetables are soft and browned very lightly, if at all, about 20 minutes. Use a lid or a splash of water if it's coloring too much before getting soft. Turn the mirepoix out onto a plate and set it aside to cool completely. Grate ½ teaspoon zest from the lime and set it aside.

Chop the cod into ¼-inch dice, place it in a medium bowl, and season it with ¾ teaspoon salt and some grindings of black pepper. In the bowl of a food processor, combine a quarter of the fish with the cream and pulse until smooth, scraping down the sides as needed. Add the fish puree back to the bowl of chopped fish along with the cooled vegetable mixture, cilantro, jalapeño, lime zest, 1½ cups bread crumbs, and 2 of the eggs. Stir with your hands and squeeze through your fingers to mix everything really well, then heat a skillet to medium, add a teaspoon of oil and fry a little piece for tasting. Adjust as needed and when you have the seasoning right, begin breading: Beat the remaining 2 eggs in a wide, shallow bowl, put the flour in another bowl, and the remaining 2 cups bread crumbs in a third. Have a baking sheet ready to receive the breaded cakes. Pat the fish mixture down in the bowl, smooth the top, divide it in half, then separate each half into 3 parts to make sixths. Scoop up half of one of the sixths, form it into a ball with your hands, flatten it into a patty, and place it in the flour. Turn the patty to coat, shake off the excess, and then place it in the eggs. Turn it to coat completely, let excess egg drip off, and then place it in the crumbs. Coat it completely with crumbs, set it on the baking sheet, and repeat with the remaining mixture until you have 12 fishcakes. Refrigerate them for 20 minutes to 6 hours before cooking.

When you're ready, heat a skillet to medium-high and heat the oven to warm for holding one batch of fishcakes as you fry the rest. Add ¼ inch of oil to the skillet and then as many fishcakes as will fit in a single layer. Fry, adjusting the heat as needed, until one side of the cakes is golden brown, about 4 minutes. Turn and brown the other side. Peek into one of the cakes to be sure it's cooked through and then keep the batch warm in the oven while you fry the rest. Right before serving, squeeze lime juice over the fishcakes.

* *Replace part of the fish amount with diced and seasoned scallops or shrimp or boiled and picked crabmeat.*
* *Use chervil, chives, and/or tarragon instead of cilantro and skip the jalapeño.*
* *Make tiny fishcakes to fry and pass as an aperitivo.*

CHICKEN AL MATTONE

Cutting the meat from chicken leg bones takes some practice and a little x-ray vision, which, believe me, you do have. Believe me further that it is worth the effort because, once deboned, chicken al mattone sports super-crisp skin and moist, juicy meat, is easy to cook, and lets you use a brick in your kitchen! If you don't have a brick, it's fine, you can use a heavy pan. Whichever weight you use, it must be slightly smaller than the skillet you are cooking in: if it fits too closely, the chicken will get steamy and pale rather than brown and crisped. For public health and safety, I wrap the weight—brick or smaller skillet—in foil.

Makes 6 servings

6 bone-in, skin-on chicken legs (drumstick and thigh together)

2 teaspoons salt

Freshly ground black pepper

Leaves from 1 or 2 fresh rosemary sprigs (optional)

Crushed red pepper flakes (optional)

Cooking oil, olive or vegetable

Using your sharpest knife, preferably a thin-bladed boning knife, cut first through the skin and tendons around the drumstick ankle and then position the chicken leg on a cutting board with the skin side down and the elbow joint away from you. There are two bones; you can see the ends of them right and left, and they meet at that elbow. You want to expose the bones before cutting them out, so start slicing into the meat, following along where the bones run. Once you see them, use your non-knife-holding fingers to open up the cut and work your knife in along to the sides of the bones. Slip the blade all the way through under the drumstick bone, near the elbow, so that the meat is below the blade and the bone is above it, with the sharp edge facing away from the elbow. Slice out, past the end of the bone, and then repeat on the thigh side so that the meat is now attached only, or mostly, at the elbow. Continue cutting meat from bone and, when you are able to, bring the two bone ends together and cut the meat free from the elbow. Check to see if any bits of bone or hard cartilage need trimming away and then repeat with the remaining legs. Sprinkle the legs with the salt, being a bit more generous on the skin side, and grind on some black pepper. Save the bones for brodo-making (page 42). Press a sprinkling of rosemary leaves and red pepper flakes onto the skin sides, if desired.

Heat a skillet to medium-high. Depending on the size of your skillet and how many legs you plan to cook at once, you may need to heat two. Cooking in two batches in the same skillet works fine, too; just hold the first batch in a warm oven while you fry the second. Have your weight ready.

Add 2 tablespoons oil to the skillet and lay in the chicken legs, skin side down. They can be touching each other a little—they'll shrink as they cook. Put the weight on top. After 4 minutes, unweight and check to see if the skin is getting too brown or not brown enough and adjust the heat accordingly. Replace the weight, making sure it's pushing everything down, and continue cooking until the skin is well browned, 8 to 10 minutes. The meat should be

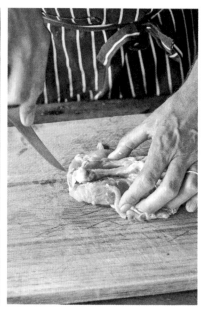

mostly cooked by this point as well. To finish it, turn the legs over, lowering the heat if it seems too hot, but *do not* re-cover or the skin will lose its crispness. Tip off some of the fat if it seems ridiculous, but again, do not replace the weight. They are done when cooked through, about an additional 4 minutes.

* *Mashed potatoes, squash, or roots are nice backgrounds for chicken al mattone, and fried herb salsa (page 250) is always a good idea, or pass a bowl of mostarda (page 269) or pickled peaches (page 268).*
* *Chicken, and other meats, have become too cheap. In 1919 it took an American worker two and a half hours to earn enough money to buy a chicken; these days it would take less than fifteen minutes of labor. I'm sorry, but I have seen a chicken, a live one, and that is too cheap. By my back-of-an-envelope calculations, that 1919 chicken would cost about forty dollars at today's rates, so I think we need to do what they no doubt did back then: buy a well-raised, whole chicken, pay the higher price— its real worth—but make it last: get a couple of meals out of it and save all the bones for soup. That, and cook and eat more lentils, beans, and chickpeas.*

CHOU FARCI, OR CHICKEN STUFFED ALL UP IN A CABBAGE LEAF

Typically, especially in colder months, I use pork or duck or both for stuffing cabbage leaves. This version, made with chicken, buttered bread, and lots of herbs, is light and good, especially with a fresh summer tomato sauce.

(Annoying but true: it's better if the meat is hand-chopped. It's hard to do, and a little dangerous, so probably forget about it and get some ground meat. If you can't forget about it, bribe your butcher to do it, or . . . ask him to show you how to do it yourself. In addition to your sharpest chef's knife or cleaver, use this trick: spread the boneless and skinless chicken thighs on a baking sheet and freeze for 1 or 2 hours. They should be very firm, but not frozen hard. Slice this way, then slice that way, then dice, and then give a final chop.)

Makes 6 servings

4 tablespoons (½ stick) unsalted butter

1 yellow onion, diced

Salt

2 garlic cloves, finely chopped

Leaves from 6 to 8 thyme sprigs, chopped (about 2 tablespoons)

Leaves from 1 marjoram sprig, chopped (about 1 teaspoon)

¼ cup white wine

2 ounces stale, crustless bread, torn (an orange-size chunk pulled into raspberry-size pieces)

1 large savoy or green cabbage head (about 2 pounds)

½ bunch chard, leaves torn from the stems, washed

1¼ pounds ground dark meat chicken

Freshly ground black pepper

1 tablespoon chopped parsley

2 tablespoons toasted pine nuts (page 9; optional)

2 tablespoons cooking oil, olive or vegetable

Melt the butter in a skillet over high heat. When it foams, add the onion and ¼ teaspoon salt. Stir until it gets going, then turn to medium and cook, stirring occasionally, until soft but not browned (a little is okay), about 15 minutes. Add the garlic, thyme, and marjoram and cook, stirring, until the garlic smells good. Raise the heat and add the wine. Bubble for a couple of minutes to reduce by half, then mix with the torn bread and set aside.

Bring a pot of water large enough to hold the entire head of cabbage to a boil. Remove and discard any brown or dark green outer leaves from the cabbage. With a paring knife, cut out and remove the core—it should come out as a cone shape and will expose the thick-ribbed ends of the leaves. Add 2 teaspoons salt to the water and slip the cabbage in. Using a spider or tongs, dunk the head under and turn it so that the air can escape from between the leaves and allow it to sink. Boil until tender, 5 to 10 minutes—the only way to check this is to pull off a leaf and taste: tender, but not falling apart, is the aim. Remove the cabbage from the pot and allow it to cool and drain, cut side down. Carefully pull off 14 of the outermost leaves to stuff, keeping them as whole as possible (this is 2 more than you need, but the extras may come in handy later to patch ripped leaves). With a paring knife, trim out the thick-

est part of each leaf's center rib and discard. Chop the remaining cabbage into ¼-inch pieces and set aside. Now boil the chard, adding an extra pinch of salt, until it is tender, about 4 minutes. Let it drain and cool, chop it roughly, and set it aside.

Put the ground chicken in a large mixing bowl and season it with ½ teaspoon salt, plenty of pepper, and the parsley. Add the onion-bread mixture, the chopped cabbage and chard, and the pine nuts, if you're using them. Squeeze the mixture through your fingers to combine everything really well, and then fry a little piece for tasting. Adjust as needed, and when you have the seasoning right, pat the mixture down in the bowl, smooth the top, and divide it into quarters. Lay out 3 of the cabbage leaves. Form 3 patties from one of the quarters of filling and set each patty in the center of a cabbage leaf. Fold the cabbage around the filling, like wrapping a gift—a tricky-to-wrap, round gift made of chicken. Set the stuffed leaves aside, smooth sides up, marveling at their verdancy and your handiwork, and then wrap up the rest. The stuffed leaves can be cooked right away or refrigerated for up to a day to cook later.

To cook, heat the oven to 450°F. Heat a cast-iron pan to medium-high, add 2 tablespoons oil, and then carefully place in the bundles, smooth side down. (You'll need two pans or two batches if you're cooking all 12.) When they are browned, about 5 minutes, turn them over and put the pan in the hot oven to cook them through, another 5 minutes or so. Check for doneness by peeking into one from the rough side. Serve, pretty side up, atop spoonfuls of summer marinara (page 267) or with plain boiled rice or spring onion champ (page 202).

* *Even when I know we're not going to be able to eat them all that night, I will often cook the whole batch of bundles—sliced cold the next day with a small salad and a dab of mustard, they make a no-effort, awfully nice lunch, especially with a cold glass of something white and dry.*
* *Replace the thyme and marjoram with a couple tablespoons roughly chopped cilantro and season the chicken with 1 teaspoon each ground cumin, coriander, and turmeric, ½ teaspoon each ground fennel and paprika, and 1 or 2 cloves, ground. (Or, if you have some curry powder that you like, use 1½ tablespoons of it instead.)*
* *For a vegetarian version, replace the chicken with the same amount of mushrooms, cleaned and sautéed in butter and coarsely chopped.*

YOGURT-FRIED BLACK PEPPER CHICKEN

My son Liam asked me what I would do if we were invited to someone's house for dinner and they set a bucket of fried chicken on the table. "Ask for a thigh," I surprised him by saying. He was thinking, hoping even, that I would upturn the table in a sustainable, organic, slow-food frenzy. Or maybe he was just wishing I'd make fried chicken more often.

Using yogurt to coat chicken before dredging it in flour is just like using buttermilk, only easier, because, if you're like me, you already have yogurt on hand. A spicy amount of black pepper kicks up the slightly sweet, tangy batter.

Makes 6 servings

2½ pounds boneless, skinless chicken thighs and/or drumsticks

2 teaspoons salt

Freshly ground black pepper

¼ cup plain yogurt

At least 1 quart oil for frying

2 cups all-purpose flour for dredging

Season the chicken with the salt and a lot of pepper. Set it aside at room temperature for 15 minutes, then coat it completely with the yogurt. Pour the flour into a cake pan or wide shallow bowl. Heat the oven to low for keeping batch 1 warm while you fry batch 2. In a deep skillet or pot, heat 3 to 4 inches of oil until a little bit of yogurt rolled with flour on your fingers and dropped into the oil floats and sizzles, but not alarmingly—around 350°F on a fry thermometer.

Place several pieces of chicken in the flour, coat them completely, shake off the excess, and lower them into the hot oil. Repeat until half the chicken is in the oil. Fry it to golden brown, turning it once if necessary, for approximately 12 minutes—check for doneness by cutting into a piece and peeking to be sure it's cooked through. With a spider, lift the chicken out of the oil, drain it on a rack or crumpled paper, and keep it warm in the oven (without the paper, if that's what you're using) while you fry the remaining pieces.

* *Chicken-frying oil cannot really be reused and should be discarded.*

TURKEY BREAST SCALOPPINE GRILLED
WITH HERBS: A RALLYING CRY

This would be a great recipe if it weren't so hard to find turkey that isn't either a big ol' frozen Butterball or a loaf sitting in the deli case ready to slice. So this is *not* a recipe but a plea to butchers and farmers: more turkey! We should be able to buy and cook fresh turkey, not just in November but year-round. Other countries seem to, but here it tends to be Thanksgiving or sandwich or not at all. Imagine, though, the comfort and satisfaction that would be ours if we could buy some turkey thighs to braise up tender and flavorful or to grind, along with the drumstick meat, for excellent meatballs and ragù. Turkey bones, as every day-after-Thanksgiving cook knows, make the best stock, and wouldn't it be nice to buy some slices of fresh turkey breast—little scaloppini to grill with lots of herbs, or to flour and pan-fry and eat with capers, lemon, and hot butter?

I propose a campaign for the turkey. Not quite like Benjamin Franklin's demands that the turkey replace the bald eagle as our national emblem, nor Calvin Trillin's that spaghetti carbonara replace turkey at the Thanksgiving table, though I like those ideas, and both might, in their own ways, support mine. Go to your butcher, to your market, and ask for turkey parts to cook. Demand them, in a polite way, and together, we can bring turkey into the culinary flock as it so deserves to be.

DUCK COOKED TWO WAYS

Pan-Roasted Breast with Sweet Spices and Leg Braised with Orange Zest and Bay Leaves

When faced with a whole duck to cook, not separate parts but the whole bird, one has two choices—either roast it as is or cut the breasts and legs from the carcass and cook them separately. I chose the latter when my colleague Jean-Pierre presented me with a wild duck he'd shot himself. I was impressed that he hunted his own birds and flattered that he gave me one. My then-seven-year-old son Milo was *very* impressed with JP for owning and using a gun.

"A gun?" he asked, wide-eyed. "Jean-Pierre has a gun? A real gun? That he shoots?"

Duck he'd had before, but the only talk Milo ever heard about guns was that they were dangerous and to be avoided, even toy ones.

"I guess so. I think he uses it for hunting wild pigs sometimes, and I know he used it to shoot this duck."

"Can I see it?" Milo asked, his face shining, his voice solemn, almost whispering.

"Sure," I said, reaching into the bag for the duck, but stopped by the look on my son's face. It wasn't a dead duck that he wanted to see. That look was not quite one of disgust or contempt or disappointment, but it was close. A look that didn't make me wish I could pull a rifle out of that paper bag—my own rifle, to fieldstrip, oil, load, and fire—but almost did. I knew I could cook duck, could skillfully cut the breasts and legs from the carcass, cook them each to a turn, and serve them with complex, elegant sauces. Undeniably cool as that is, it could not possibly compare, for my seven-year-old boy, to gun, bullet, trigger, and muzzle flash. Milo started to turn away. I needed something.

"One time I tangled with a duck, and I ended up with six stitches," I bragged. It was true. I'd been chasing a duck across a gravel yard, and it stopped short.

"A duck'll do that" is what I remember my dad saying on the way to the doctor as I tried not to think about the gash and blood.

Milo looked at me with some disbelief, but not so much—a dad can tell—that he wouldn't ask me for gory details later.

Makes 6 servings

3 duck legs (drumstick and thigh together)

Salt

Freshly ground black pepper

3 duck breasts

1 teaspoon coriander seeds

½ teaspoon fennel seeds

½ teaspoon black peppercorns

4 whole cloves

2 allspice berries

4 bay leaves

Cooking oil, olive or vegetable

1 yellow onion, roughly chopped

1 carrot, roughly chopped

2 celery stalks, roughly chopped

2 garlic cloves, skins left on, cut in half

3 thyme sprigs

3 parsley sprigs

1 orange

½ cup white wine

2 cups chicken stock (page 44) or water

The morning of, or day before, cooking the duck, cut through the skin and tendons around the ankle-ends of the legs—this will provide a neat look when the skin shrinks during cooking. Though much of the fat will render during cooking, if it seems excessive around the edges, trim some off, but don't cut away any of the soon-to-be-delicious skin. Season the duck legs with a scant 2 teaspoons salt and several cranks of black pepper and refrigerate them for 6 hours or overnight. Bring to room temperature before cooking.

With a sharp knife, trim excess fat, but not skin, from around the perimeter of the breast. Score the skin, cutting just through the fat and to, but not into, the flesh beneath it. Score a crosshatch with the cuts about ½ inch apart. Trim any silver skin and wiggly bits from the flesh side. Toast the coriander, fennel, black pepper, cloves, and allspice in a dry skillet until fragrant and starting to wiggle. Using a mortar and pestle or a spice mill, grind the spices to powder with 2 of the bay leaves. Season the duck breasts with ¾ teaspoon salt and the spice mixture, hitting the skin side more heavily than the flesh side. Set aside at room temperature for half an hour to a couple hours while you braise the legs.

Heat the oven to 450°F.

Heat a skillet over high and add 3 tablespoons oil and then the onion, carrot, and celery. Stir until it gets going, then turn to medium and cook, stirring occasionally, until softened and lightly browned, about 15 minutes. Add the garlic, thyme, parsley, the remaining 2 bay leaves, and strips of zest from half the orange and cook a minute more. Add the wine and juice of half the orange and bring to a simmer while you eat the other half. Place the duck legs in, skin side down, and nestle them into the skillet. Add the stock or water so that the liquid nearly covers them. Bring to a simmer, cover the skillet with foil or a lid, put it in the oven, and reduce the heat to 350°F. (If you are cooking more legs than will fit in a skillet, braise them in a casserole or baking dish instead.) After 20 minutes, turn the duck legs over so that the skin side is up (try to handle the legs by the drumstick ends so that you don't tear up the skin too much). Into a bowl set under a sieve, tip off enough of the liquid so that all the skin is above the waterline, but there's still some juice underneath (reserve the liquid in the bowl; a small, deep-sided one will make the degreasing process easier later). You may have to shift things around a bit so that all the skin is exposed and can get browned and crispy. Return the duck legs to the oven and cook until they are very tender and well browned, 45 minutes to an hour more.

To check for doneness, grab a drumstick bone with tongs and the end of the thighbone with your other hand and a kitchen towel. Bend the ends toward each other, and if it feels like you could easily make them touch, it's done. If the joint still feels springy, cook the legs more. If the liquid has evaporated and only fat remains with the vegetables, add back some of the reserved liquid. If the skin is getting very dark and the meat does not yet seem tender, re-cover the skillet and cook a little longer.

When the legs are done, set them aside and strain the remaining contents of the skillet into the bowl with the reserved liquid. Discard the vegetables and herbs (or push them through the sieve with the back of a spoon to thicken and sweeten the juices) and set the liquid aside for 5 minutes to allow the fat to rise to the top. With a small ladle, skim off the collected fat and discard it (or save it for potatoes al mattone, page 223, or for toasting rustic croutons). Separate each thigh from its drumstick by cutting through the joint where they meet, return them to the braising liquid—skin side up—and set them aside while you cook the breasts.

Heat a skillet to medium-high and add 1 tablespoon cooking oil and then the duck breasts, skin side down. Lower to medium—the goal here is to achieve browned crispy skin over cooked luxurious fat, so . . . not too fast (browned skin, but unrendered fat) or too slow (fat rendered, but skin pale and soft). Get the heat right so that the skin is coloring and a lot of fat is accumulating in the pan—signs of proper rendering. When the skin is mahogany and much of the fat has melted away, turn the breasts over to cook the flesh side. Tip off all but a film of fat and put the skillet in the oven.

The breasts will be done when they feel firm as you press them and the meat is still pink in the center—about 7 minutes, but make an incision on the flesh side and sneak a peek to be sure. Remove the breasts from the skillet and let them rest in a warm place for 5 minutes while you bring the pan with the legs to a simmer and put it in the oven to reheat. Slice the duck breasts across and serve them with the legs and some of the hot braising liquid.

* *Serve with . . . carrot puree (page 196) or white root puree (page 236) or spring onion champ (page 202) or creamy corn polenta (page 208), and roasted or boiled vegetables of the season. Pass fried herb salsa (page 250).*

LAMB SHOULDER BRAISED WITH MOROCCAN SPICES AND GREEN OLIVES

Back on the farm in New Jersey, where I grew up, we had a big garden, laying hens, and a little flock of sheep. The vegetables and eggs I liked well enough, but eating lamb . . . not so much. It annoyed me when my mom said it was because I was "sensitive," and it annoys me even more to now realize that—as she was about so many things—maybe she was right. I *am* sensitive, but not about lamb—I enjoy eating it very much and in every way from shank to rack, spring to mutton. There are many who don't: lamb can have a distinctive pungency, especially from older animals, that American eaters have grown suspicious of. At the restaurant, we grill young lamb whose sweet, clean flavor consistently makes converts, but I also like to eat the more mature, flavorful meat, like that often served in Indian and Middle Eastern restaurants. This Morocco-tinged braise, full of spice and savor, will bring everyone to the table.

Makes 6 servings

2 pounds lamb shoulder, cut into chunks

Salt

Spice mixture: 1 teaspoon ground turmeric; ½ teaspoon each crushed saffron threads, ground ginger, and ground black pepper; ⅛ teaspoon each ground cinnamon and grated nutmeg

Cooking oil, olive or vegetable

½ cup white wine

1 yellow onion, diced

1 large carrot, halved lengthwise and sliced

4 garlic cloves, sliced or roughly chopped

Small handful cilantro leaves and stems, chopped (about ½ cup)

Small handful parsley leaves, chopped (about ½ cup)

4 cups chicken stock (page 44; or lamb stock or water)

½ cup green olives

1 batch cooked couscous (page 141)

Harissa (page 261) or chermoula (page 259)

At least an hour and as much as a day before cooking, season the lamb with 1½ teaspoons salt and the spice mixture. Bring the lamb to room temperature before cooking and heat the oven to 400°F. Heat a skillet to medium-high and add 2 tablespoons cooking oil and then the lamb pieces, filling the skillet but not crowding it—you may need to do the browning in two batches. Turn the lamb to brown all sides, but not right away: moving it too soon prevents the nice caramelizing you are looking for. Adjust the heat so that the meat gets browned but the skillet stays unburned—10 minutes, total, should do it.

Set the lamb pieces aside on a plate, pour off the grease, and, unless the skillet looks too dark and burned, add the wine to deglaze, stirring and scraping up all the sweet and flavorful bits over medium heat. When all is dissolved and dislodged, pour the deglazing liquid into a bowl and set it aside. (If the skillet was in fact too burned, just wash it out and skip the deglazing step, adding the wine later when the lamb goes back in.) Add 2 tablespoons cooking oil (or some of the poured-off grease), the onion, carrot, garlic, and herbs to the skillet and stir for 3 or 4 minutes. Turn the vegetables out into a shallow baking dish (or just leave them in the skillet, if all the meat and liquid will fit), add the stock to the skillet with the reserved deglazing liquid, and bring it to a boil. Put the olives and the browned lamb atop the vegetables, cover with foil, and put it in the oven. After 10 minutes, reduce the heat to 325°F and cook until the meat is very tender, about 2 hours. Uncover and set the skillet or dish atilt so the liquid runs to one side and you can skim off any excess fat. Add more hot stock or water if it needs to be juicier and serve with couscous, harissa or chermoula, roasted or boiled vegetables or sautéed greens, and a warning about olive pits.

SPICY GROUND PORK WITH GINGER, LIME, PEPPERS, AND GREEN BEANS

Not that I need any more encouragement to cook and eat ground pork, delicious as it is, but whenever I talk to my pig-farming friends, they always mention wanting to sell more ground meat. It allows them to make some money from the in-between bits, not just the chops, hams, and bellies. More plump sausages and tasty porky sauces? Well, all right.

This recipe for ground pork brings in some of the flavors I love in Vietnamese cookery. In summer, I sometimes add red or yellow peppers cut in strips, and in winter I like to substitute broccoli for the green beans and add roasted slices of Delicata squash. Serve with romaine lettuce leaves, coarsely chopped, and plain boiled rice.

Makes 6 servings

1 pound ground pork

Salt

1 teaspoon sugar

Freshly ground black pepper

2 garlic cloves, pounded with a pinch of salt

2 teaspoons minced or grated ginger (about 1 inch)

2 teaspoons coriander seeds, toasted and ground (see page 9)

Crushed red pepper flakes

1 teaspoon fish sauce

½ teaspoon rice wine vinegar

(or any unflavored vinegar)

Cooking oil, olive or vegetable

1 yellow onion, thinly sliced pole to pole

1 red or yellow pepper, stemmed, seeded, and cut into ¼-inch strips

1 pound green beans, topped

¾ cup chicken stock (page 44; or pork stock or water)

Handful cilantro leaves and stems, chopped

1 or 2 limes, cut into wedges

In a large bowl, combine the pork, ½ teaspoon salt, the sugar, black pepper, garlic paste, ginger, coriander, hot pepper, fish sauce, vinegar, and 1 tablespoon oil and mix thoroughly. Heat a skillet to medium, add a dot of oil, and fry a little patty of the sausage mixture. Taste and add more of whatever you like—spicier? fishier? sweeter? more salt? Mix and do another test patty.

Bring a pot of salted water to a boil for cooking the beans. Reheat the skillet to medium-high and add 2 tablespoons oil, then the sausage, spreading it to cover the surface of the skillet. Let it cook, undisturbed, to get nice and brown before turning it to brown the other side.

When just cooked through, set the sausage aside on a plate, add more oil to the skillet if needed, then add the onion and red pepper strips with ¼ teaspoon salt. Cook, stirring occasionally, until they have wilted but still have a little crunch, about 10 minutes. Meanwhile, cook the green beans in the boiling water until tender. If they are done before the onion and pepper, set them aside on a plate, or just add them into the skillet if the timing is right. Add the sausage to the skillet and the stock or water for stewiness, bring to a simmer, taste, adjust, and serve sprinkled with cilantro. Pass lime wedges to squeeze over.

*   *Add coconut milk, up to a whole can, with the stock or water for creamy rich tropicality.*

PORK BELLY BRAISED WITH FENNEL SEEDS AND SWEET WINE

When you do something long enough, you find yourself speaking jargon that you're not even aware of. Or at least I think that was the problem one evening at the restaurant as I tried to explain what pork belly was. A waiter relayed the question from a guest, and at first I was surprised that *he* didn't seem to know, and second, surprised at how difficult it was to explain it to him—if you know something really well and have been around and about it forever, its obviousness can become the very obstacle to describing it effectively. Out we went to the dining room, the waiter and I, puzzled for different reasons.

"Is it an organ? I don't like tripe. It's the stomach, isn't it?" one of the guests asked, speaking fast and looking worried.

"No," I said, recalling now that my usual description of pork belly was dependent on rubbing my hands on my own belly, and realizing further that performing that gesture tableside could be misleading, possibly giving an impression that mine was the belly to be braised with fennel, bay leaves, and Muscat de Beaumes-de-Venise.

"It's the belly," I went on, stating only what was already known.

"Outside," I added, to no effect, arms raising and spreading, despite my resolve, and trying to come up with something more but hindered by not quite getting what there was to not get. *It's the pig's freaking belly*, I wanted to shout, *the part with nipples that drags in the mud!*

They were waiting; the waiter was, too. Slowly, involuntarily, my hands were moving toward my belly.

"Bacon!" I nearly shouted, turning a few heads at a nearby table. "It's what *bacon* is made from, what bacon *is*."

I sounded like an idiot, but they got it and looked relieved. Bacon—always so helpful. The waiter poured wine, table conversation restarted, and I walked back toward the kitchen, victoriously rubbing my belly.

2½-pound slab pork belly, skin removed (ask/bribe the butcher to do it)

1 tablespoon salt

1 tablespoon fennel seeds, toasted and coarsely ground (see page 9)

4 bay leaves, ground with the fennel seeds

Freshly ground black pepper

1 yellow onion, thickly sliced

2 carrots, thickly sliced

2 celery stalks, thickly sliced

6 thyme sprigs

6 parsley sprigs

4 garlic cloves, skins left on, cracked

3 strips orange zest

⅓ cup muscat wine or other sweet wine such as Marsala, Madeira, or sweet Riesling

The day before you plan to cook the pork belly, sprinkle it with the salt, fennel seeds, bay leaves, and some black pepper and rub them in. Refrigerate.

Next day, let the pork come to room temperature while you heat the oven to 450°F. Put the onion, carrots, celery, thyme, parsley, garlic, and orange zest in a baking dish that will fit the meat snugly. Place the pork belly on top, fat side down, pour in the wine and 1 cup hot water, cover with foil, and put in the oven. Lower the heat to 275°F and cook for 2 hours. Uncover, flip the belly over, and cook until it is well browned, and a knife blade slips in and out of the meat with very little resistance, about 1 hour more. Add water if all the liquid has evaporated—it should come halfway up the thickness of the pork belly—and re-cover with the foil if the pork is getting too dark before it's cooked tender.

Set the pork belly aside and strain the liquid, discarding the aromatics and, after letting it settle for 5 minutes, skimming off the fat. If you're not eating right away, put the belly back in the dish with the liquid and let it cool. Either reheat it as is in a 425°F oven or slice and brown it in a skillet, spooning some of the hot cooking liquid on the serving platter.

* *Classic with beans and greens or a green salad.*
* *Serve belly slices with rolled pork loin slices (page 183) for a glorious pig-out.*

ROLLED PORK LOIN ROAST STUFFED WITH OLIVES AND HERBS

Of course, you can just roast a chunk of pork loin and spoon tapenade over it, but when you stuff the tapenade *inside* the roast, it will look all swirled and magical when sliced. It's not that hard to do, really—two strategic cuts, a smear, a row of knotted strings—more basic butchery than brain surgery.

Makes 6 servings

2-pound boneless pork loin roast

½ teaspoon salt

Freshly ground black pepper

⅔ cup olives, pitted and finely chopped (Niçoise, Picholine, Lucques, and/or Castelvetrano)

2 tablespoons capers (salt-packed and very well soaked to desalinate, or brined capers rinsed well)

1 garlic clove, pounded with a pinch of salt

1 teaspoon finely chopped rosemary or sage leaves

1 tablespoon chopped thyme leaves

2 tablespoons chopped parsley

¼ cup good olive oil

1 tablespoon cooking oil, olive or vegetable

Set the loin on a cutting board with one of the short, cut ends facing you. With a sharp knife, make a lengthwise horizontal cut, about a third of the way up one of the long sides, like asymmetrically splitting open a hot dog bun. Don't cut all the way through, but nearly—far enough so that you can open up the roast like a book. If you started on the right, the left side will now be twice as thick as the right. At the hinge where they meet, make another horizontal cut midway up the left (thicker) side, so that you can open the roast again, like a magazine gatefold. Sprinkle the pork all over with the salt and pepper and set it aside.

Heat the oven to 425°F and make the stuffing by mixing all the remaining ingredients together (except the cooking oil). Spread the stuffing over the cut

side of the pork loin, then roll it up and back into shape. Using cotton string, bind the roast with six little string belts.

Heat a skillet to high, add the cooking oil, and then carefully lay in the pork roast. Brown the roast on all sides and then put the skillet in the oven. Roast until it is just cooked through, about 20 minutes, then remove it from the pan and let it rest on a platter in a warm place for 10 minutes. Remove the strings, slice, and serve.

* *Serve with slices of braised pork belly (page 180) for a glorious pig-out.*
* *Good served alongside so many things (see the "Alongside" chapter, page 193).*

CAST-IRON PAN ROAST

Let's say you want a nice charred roast to slice for dinner. It's raining and dark and chilly out there, and you need to warm things up, but you can't grill because . . . it's raining and so dark and chilly out there. Or you're simply out of charcoal. A cast-iron pan, heated till it's just short of furious, will, with a little smoke and spatter, be your grill tonight.

A lamb leg roast will work very well. Rib eye and New York steak cut very thick, like 4 or even 5 inches, are prime beef cuts for cast-iron pan cooking. Go-tos like tri-tip and top sirloin are less spendy and no less appealing. Skip the dreaded, bafflingly named London broil (usually top round) that Dad used to burn on the gas grill, which is, after all these years, still tough and disappointing. Pork leg, if you can find it, extra carefully cooked and thinly sliced, can be very tasty, especially with a nice sauce to mitigate any dryness. Otherwise the fancier, commoner pork loin roast, with or without rib bones, is excellent this way.

Makes 6 servings

2½-pound beef tri-tip roast, or pork loin or leg roast, or lamb leg roast

1½ teaspoons salt

Freshly ground black pepper

2 tablespoons cooking oil, olive or vegetable

Heat the oven to 450°F.

An hour before you plan to cook it, season the roast with the salt and plenty of black pepper and leave it out at room temperature. Heat a skillet to high, add the oil, and then carefully put in the roast. Leave it in place to brown for 4 or 5 minutes, then turn it to brown another side. Turn it onto the last side in need of browning and put the skillet in the oven to roast to your desired doneness.

Poke the roast with a finger, and when it feels like it's firming up, make a small cut with a sharp knife to take a peek inside to see if it's done the way you like it. Remember that it will continue cooking a degree as it sits out of the oven. Remove the roast to a platter and put it in a warm spot to rest for 10 minutes before slicing it thinly across the grain.

* *Pass a bowl of béarnaise, fried herb salsa, salsa rossa, tomato vinaigrette, romesco, caponatina, chermoula, mostarda (see the "Sauces" chapter).*
* *Good served alongside so many things (see the "Alongside" chapter).*

BRAISED AND GRILLED OR GRIDDLED SHORT RIBS

This one is a throwback to a throwback sort of place, San Francisco's Bix Restaurant, the first kitchen I ever cooked in. The chef, Gordon Drysdale, served up luxe American supper club fare to diners drinking martinis in plush booths and he hired me as entry-level garde manger. The kitchen was a small behind-the-scene galley, but the bar was big and my station was at one end of it, terrifyingly open to the soaring, Deco dining room. I wore a paper toque, ripped and taped up to fit my big head, which I was clearly in over, and tried hard to open oysters and torch crèmes brûlées without shedding blood or setting my hat on fire. With his solid retro menus, Gordon taught me classic after classic, and this way of braising and then griddling beef short ribs is one of my favorites. I can still smell the butter as it skittered and foamed across the flattop, browning a little before the split short ribs were set there to finish. A plate of these crisped, tender ribs with a fluff of mashed potatoes and spoonful of peas, preceded by an herb-scattered romaine salad wedge and followed with a slice of Boston cream pie . . . that was Bix.

Beef short ribs are champion braisers. Their flavor is between rib eye and skirt steak, and, in fact, short ribs come from right between the rib eye and the skirt. Fatty and tough to start, they cook up to a sticky, tasty tenderness, make their own sauce, and because they are pretty rich, you don't need to serve a lot. You might want to cook some extra, though—short ribs make some of the best leftovers (as in agnolotti, page 37).

Makes 6 servings

3 teaspoons salt	3 ground bay leaves
Freshly ground black pepper	4 pounds short ribs
1 teaspoon fennel seeds, toasted and ground (see page 9)	2 onions, halved, each half cut into quarters
5 whole cloves, toasted and ground	1 large carrot, cut into thick slices
3 allspice berries, toasted and ground	3 celery stalks, cut into thick slices

1 medium tomato or half a
14.5-ounce can whole peeled
tomatoes, cut into chunks

6 thyme sprigs

6 parsley sprigs

2 whole bay leaves

3 big garlic cloves, skins left on,
halved

Crushed red pepper flakes

½ cup red wine (or white)

3 cups hot chicken stock (page 44;
or beef stock or water)

1½ teaspoons red wine vinegar

Cooking oil, olive or vegetable, or
butter (optional)

Combine the salt and black pepper with the ground fennel, cloves, allspice, and bay. Use the mixture to season the short ribs.

Cover and refrigerate overnight (or leave at room temperature for at least an hour).

Next day, take them out of the fridge to come to room temperature. Heat the oven to 450°F. Place the short ribs in a roasting pan or casserole in a single layer, bone side down, leaving space between them for better browning. Roast until they are nicely colored and smelling beefy, about 30 minutes. Set the ribs aside and add the onions, carrot, celery, and tomato to the pan. Stir, then roast the aromatics until nicely browned and smelling vegetable-y, about 10 minutes. Pour off the fat, scatter the thyme, parsley, bay leaves, garlic, and a pinch of crushed red pepper flakes over the aromatics, and then arrange the ribs on top, bone side up this time. Pour in the wine, hot stock, and vinegar; cover with foil; and return to the oven.

When the liquid starts to bubble, after about 15 minutes, loosen the foil at one edge to allow steam to escape and lower the heat to 300°F. Cook until the meat is very tender and pulling away from the bones, about 2 hours. It's best to allow the short ribs to cool in their liquid, but that takes a while and can be skipped if timing demands. Lift the short ribs from the pan and set them aside while you strain the liquid, let it settle, and skim off the fat.

At this point you could just reunite meat and juice, reheat and eat, but oh, please try this: Cut or pull the bones off and let the ribs cool completely. Cut them in half lengthwise and either brush them with oil and grill over hot coals until browned and crispy, or get them that way with butter in a hot cast-iron pan. To serve, put a little of the hot braising juice on a platter and arrange the short ribs on top.

* *Serve with potato or vegetable puree (pages 196, 202, 225, 236) and passed bowls of fried herb salsa (page 250), mostarda (page 266), or horseradish crème fraîche (page 248).*

ALONGSIDE

The thing about side dishes is that they really aren't, or shouldn't be, off to the side, merely providing support for some more important part of the plate. Side dishes *are* the plate, the composition into which the meat or fish fits. Or doesn't fit . . . give me a trio of side dishes as a meal any day; it's often what I order when traveling and eating out and longing for vegetables. Side dishes, like sidemen, are better when grouped than meats could ever be—imagine a long car ride with Don Quixote, Sherlock Holmes, and Tom Sawyer . . . torture! Much better to ride with Sancho, Watson, and Huck.

Spring

CARROT PUREE WITH CARAWAY SEEDS

Since I tend to buy spices from bulk bins and store them in repurposed jars, they are not always, or maybe even ever, properly labeled. Not usually a problem—I know a spice by sight; but caraway and cumin—they really do look alike. Maybe it's time to get myself some eyeglasses, but that's how the seasoning for these carrots came about. As soon as the seeds started toasting, they sent up a signal that I'd grabbed the wrong jar, but I decided to go with it. I used much less than I would have if it were cumin, and I like it—reminds me of ducking into Jewish delis and Ukrainian diners to warm up when a cold New York winter would drag on into spring.

Makes 6 servings

1 large russet or yellow potato, peeled, halved, and cut into 1-inch slices

Salt

1½ pounds large carrots, cut into ½-inch slices

5 tablespoons butter

1 teaspoon caraway seeds, toasted and coarsely ground (see page 9)

This is a simple recipe, so I offer two methods: stewed for the deep comfort needed when Spring has yet to defeat Winter and steamed for a bright celebration of when it has.

Stewed: Boil the potato in salted water until it is fully cooked through. Pass it through a sieve or food mill into a mixing bowl and set it aside in a warm spot.

Meanwhile, put the carrots in a skillet or saucepan with a scant teaspoon salt and 2 tablespoons butter and add enough water so that most are submerged, but some are not. Bring the pan to a boil, reduce it to a simmer, and cook until the carrots are very tender, about 15 minutes—taste a piece to be sure that it is completely soft. Add water if needed, but not too much: the ideal is for the carrots to be fully cooked and sitting in just a little watery butter—you don't want to have to drain them before pureeing. Puree the carrots with their juices and

3 tablespoons butter by pushing them through a sieve, passing them through a food mill, or spinning them in a blender or food processor.

Steamed: Boil the potato in salted water until it is fully cooked through. Drain, reserving ½ cup cooking water, and pass the potato through a sieve or food mill into a mixing bowl. Set it aside in a warm spot.

Meanwhile, sprinkle the carrots with 1½ teaspoons salt, let them sit for a few minutes, and then steam them until they're very tender, about 20 minutes—taste a piece to be sure that it is completely soft. While they are still hot, puree the carrots with the butter by pushing them through a sieve, passing them through a food mill, or spinning them in a blender or food processor, adding some of the reserved potato water (or you could use milk) as needed.

To finish the dish: Stir the carrots into the potato puree with half the caraway. Taste, adjust, and add the remaining caraway if desired. Reheat carefully in a saucepan or double boiler.

FRIED POTATO AND GARLIC PUFFS

As boys, young lords of the flies, my friend and I used to play a game we called build-and-burn: we'd put together model cars and planes and then light them on fire and blow them up. It was terrible, toxic, and absolutely forbidden, so we loved it. Sometimes we had real explosive fireworks, but more often just booklets of matches to set alight and little black tablets called Magic Snakes that would hiss and smoke greasily while excreting a writhing foamy tube of dark ash. If the dough for these potato puffs is too wet, they will emit a similar, if whiter, mistake snake, so make the extra effort to keep it dry.

The dough for these puffs can be made up to twenty-four hours ahead. Refrigerate it and bring it to room temperature before frying.

Makes 6 servings

1 pound russet potatoes	2 eggs
Salt	1 garlic clove, pounded with a pinch of salt
3 tablespoons unsalted butter	
½ cup all-purpose flour	At least 1 quart oil for frying

Heat the oven to 225°F. Peel the potatoes, cut them in half lengthwise, and cut each half in 3. Boil the potatoes in well-salted water until they're completely tender but not falling apart, about 20 minutes. To check doneness, take a piece out of the pot and cut it at the thickest part. It should sort of break apart and look dry inside. Taste it to be sure, then drain the potatoes well, spread them on a baking sheet, and put them in the oven for 15 minutes to dry completely. Pass them through a sieve or food mill into a medium bowl and set them aside. If you'll be cooking the puffs as soon as the dough is ready, leave the oven on so that you can keep batches warm as you fry.

Meanwhile, make the pâte à choux: In a medium saucepan, bring ½ cup water to a boil with the butter and ¼ teaspoon salt. Add the flour all at once, turn off the heat, and stir with a wooden spoon until completely incorporated. Return the pan to very low heat and stir for a few minutes until the dough forms a ball and a cooked film begins to develop in the saucepan. Let the dough cool for a couple of minutes, and stir in one of the eggs. The dough will fly apart into seemingly irreconcilable blobs, but do not lose heart; keep stirring, and it will become one again, I promise.

Beat the other egg in a small bowl and begin to stir it in—you may not want to add all of it in the interest of dryness. Stop adding egg when the dough becomes elastic, smooth, and shiny, and then stir in the potato and garlic paste and mix thoroughly. The dough will be very sticky.

In a heavy saucepan or skillet, heat 2 to 3 inches of frying oil to 325°F, or until it is shimmery, not smoking, and a tiny dollop of the dough dropped in sizzles energetically, but does not scare you out of the kitchen. Carefully drop a walnut-size piece of dough into the oil to fry for a taster. Taste and adjust for salt and . . . more garlic? . . . cooked longer? There are two ways to proceed with frying: (1) load the dough into a pastry bag, squeeze out short lengths, and cut them off and into the oil with a knife or scissors, or (2) use two spoons to form and scrape dollops into the oil. Fry the puffs until they're golden brown, prodding them with a spider to roll them over and fry the other side as needed. Dip them out to drain on a rack or crumpled paper and keep them warm in the oven (without the paper, if that's what you're using) as you fry the rest.

* *Instead of serving the potato puffs alongside fish, meat, chicken, or beans, make them for a predinner aperitivo that you stand around eating in the kitchen while you fry the next batch.*
* *In spring, if green garlic stalks are available, thinly slice, rinse, and cook one in butter and a very little bit of salted water. When it's tender, drain and add it to the mix in place of the pounded garlic.*
* *Add chopped chives, parsley, or thyme, or Parmesan or other gratable aged cheese to the dough.*
* *Potato-puff-frying oil can be strained and saved, refrigerated, to reuse for up to a week.*

SNAP PEAS WITH SCALLIONS AND SAGE

Enthusiastically in favor of eating raw vegetables, I always buy more snap peas than I intend to cook so that the kids, as they help string pods, can crunch away and still leave enough for dinner.

Makes 6 servings

Salt

³/₄ pound snap peas, topped and strings pulled, whole or cut in half on a bias

2 tablespoons unsalted butter

1 bunch scallions, all the white and most of the green parts, thinly bias-sliced

Leaves from 4 sage sprigs

Bring a skillet of salted water to a boil and add the snap peas. Simmer until tender, 4 to 5 minutes, then drain. Set the snap peas aside and return the skillet to high heat. Add the butter, and when it stops foaming, toss in the scallions and sage leaves. Sprinkle with salt, lower to medium, and cook, stirring, until the scallions wilt and just begin to take color, 2 minutes or so. Add the snap peas back into the skillet to reheat with a couple tablespoons of water, swirling so the butter and water combine into a creamy little sauce.

SPRING ONION CHAMP

Spring onions are simply onions that have yet to form their characteristic round bulbs and papery skins. I love to roast, grill, or fry them or, as in this Irish classic, stew them in butter before folding them into mashed potatoes.

Makes 6 servings

5 russet potatoes (about 3 pounds)

Salt

½ cup half-and-half or milk, plus more as needed

8 tablespoons (1 stick) butter, plus more as needed

1 bunch spring onions or scallions, trimmed, rinsed, and all of the white and most of the green parts thinly sliced

Peel the potatoes and cut them into quarters or, if they are very big, eighths: large chunks absorb less water and yield a richer, more flavorful mash. Rinse them and cover with cold water in a saucepan. Add 1½ tablespoons salt, bring the water to a boil over high heat, then lower the heat to a simmer. Cook until the potatoes are completely tender but not falling apart, about 20 minutes. To be sure they are ready, take a wedge out of the pot and cut it at the thickest part. It should sort of break apart and look dry inside. Tasting a slice will confirm doneness and give you a sense of seasoning. Drain the potatoes and let them sit in the colander to steam and fully drain for a few minutes. Put the pan back on very low heat and add the half-and-half. Set a food mill over the pan and pass a third of the potatoes and a third of the butter through it. Repeat with the rest of the potatoes and all but 2 tablespoons of the butter.

Heat a skillet to high; add the reserved butter and, when the foaming stops, the spring onions or scallions and ½ teaspoon salt. Stir, lower the heat to medium, and cook until the onions are wilted and tender, adding a splash of water if needed to prevent any browning. Mix the onions into the potatoes, stirring just to mix completely: overmixing can result in irrevocable gumminess.

Taste and add butter and salt for flavor, half-and-half for softer texture. Serve straightaway or reheat later, adding a little more milk or half-and-half and going slowly, carefully—mashed potatoes can stick and scorch.

* *Replace the onions with a couple of carrots, diced small, simmered till tender in shallow water with salt and butter, drained if needed, and mixed into the mash.*

ARTICHOKES (OR FENNEL OR CAULIFLOWER) BAKED WITH ANCHOVIES AND BREAD CRUMBS

This is an easy way for artichoke hearts, cauliflower florets, or wedges of fennel, simply cooked, to get promoted to gratin status.

Makes 6 servings

3 cups fresh bread crumbs

Good olive oil

Salt

1 lemon

6 baseball-size artichokes (more if smaller, fewer if larger)

1 garlic clove

2-ounce can anchovies, drained

Heat the oven to 350°F.

In a medium bowl, combine the bread crumbs, 3 tablespoons oil, and a scant ½ teaspoon salt and mix well. Spread the crumbs onto a baking sheet and bake for 7 minutes (set a timer). Using a spatula, scoop the crumbs into a pile, stir them around a bit, and spread them out again. Back into the oven for 5 minutes, and repeat with the spatula. Keep baking and stirring, resetting the timer each time, until the crumbs are nearly crisp and lightly golden. Set them aside and raise the oven to 450°F.

Squeeze the lemon into a bowl of cold water big enough to hold the artichokes. Working from the bottom, snap leaves off an artichoke until the lower third of the remaining leaves are pale green to yellow. Cut off the upper green part of the leaves and peel the base and stem with a paring knife or a vegetable peeler. If the stem is very tough, cut it, or part of it, off and then split the artichoke in half lengthwise. With a spoon, scoop out and discard the hairy choke, if any, and drop the artichoke into the lemon-water to prevent discoloring while you trim and cut the remaining artichokes the same way. Drain the artichokes and cut them into wedges. Place them in a baking dish, sprinkle with salt, and stir to distribute evenly.

Pound the garlic with a pinch of salt and the anchovies to make a paste. Stir in ¼ cup oil, pour the mixture over the artichokes, and stir well to coat. Add ½ cup water, cover the dish with foil, and bake until the artichokes are tender, 25 to 30 minutes. Lower the heat to 350°F, uncover the dish, and give it a good stir, adding a little water if it's completely dry. Sprinkle the bread crumbs on top and return the dish to the oven (uncovered) for about 20 minutes to get all brown and crispy.

* *Replace the artichokes with 1 large cauliflower head, cut into florets about 1 inch in diameter, or 3 large fennel bulbs, trimmed and cut into thick wedges.*

Summer

CREAMED SWEET CORN POLENTA

I tried for years to put creamed sweet corn on the summer Chez Panisse menus, but it always seemed too creamed and too sweet while somehow being not corny enough. As a sweet-toothed kid, I didn't mind when creamed corn came from a can, but now I don't like the way it overflows, inundating real estate on the plate like silt on a floodplain. The solution was a mix of polenta for body, buttery onions for savory sweetness, and lots of corn for, well, corniness. A little dab of this golden stuff can cast a glow alongside grilled meats, and a big dollop can be the center around which ripe summer vegetables like tomatoes or peppers, green beans, or eggplant gather.

Makes 6 servings

Salt

1¼ cups polenta

4 tablespoons (½ stick) butter

4 ears sweet corn, kernels cut from the cobs

1 yellow onion, diced

½ cup heavy cream or half-and-half, plus more as needed

In a medium saucepan with a heavy bottom, bring 5 cups water to a boil over high heat. Add a scant teaspoon salt, then whisk in the polenta in a steady stream. Turn the burner down low to avoid hand-searing plops and keep stirring till the polenta thickens and the grains no longer settle but are suspended in the water, about 5 minutes. Cover loosely, turn the heat to very low, and cook, stirring often, for 30 minutes. Some kinds of polenta can take much longer—taste to be sure of doneness.

Meanwhile, heat a skillet to high and add 2 tablespoons of the butter. Swirl the pan as it foams, then add the corn kernels, ½ cup water, and ½ teaspoon salt. When it starts to bubble, lower the heat to a simmer and cook, stirring occasionally, until the corn is very tender, about 15 minutes. You may have to add another ¼ cup water if the pan dries out before the corn is fully cooked. Tip the corn out into a bowl and return the skillet to the burner over high heat. Add the remaining 2 tablespoons butter, swirl, and add the onion and ½ teaspoon salt. Turn the heat to low and cook, stirring occasionally, until the onion is very tender and translucent, not browned, about 15 minutes. Add a splash of water if needed.

When the corn has cooled a bit, put half of it, and any liquid, in a blender with the cream and whiz until smooth. Combine the resulting puree, the remaining corn kernels, and the onion with the polenta and reheat over a low flame. Taste and adjust for salt, adding more cream, half-and-half, milk, or water to get the consistency right.

ROMANO BEANS LONG-COOKED WITH GARLIC CLOVES AND SAVORY

This recipe is really for beans that have been a little too long on the bush. Whether tired or tough or just really large, beans cooked covered like this, with just oil and their own steam, become tender and deeply flavorful. They're so good that I now cook even the best green beans this way, but not the skinny French type—they are better simply boiled. I always crack some garlic cloves to long-cook with the beans—this is one time when I don't mind them browning a little. If I have savory, I'll put a few whole sprigs in the skillet, and sage works well, too.

These are very good cold or reheated, so you might want to make double if your skillet can take it.

Makes 6 servings

¼ cup olive oil

1 pound green beans

½ teaspoon salt, plus more as needed

3 or 4 garlic cloves, skins left on, cracked

3 or 4 savory sprigs

Lemon (optional)

Heat a large skillet to high and add the oil, then the green beans, salt, garlic, and savory. Stir to coat and cover with a lid. After 4 or 5 minutes, stir the beans, lower the heat to medium, and re-cover. You are aiming for beans that are browned and quite soft, so if they seem to be getting too dark and not cooking enough, turn the heat a little lower at this point. Not browning and getting soft? Higher heat. After another 4 to 5 minutes, they should be done. Taste for salt, adjust (some like a squeeze of lemon), and serve.

STEAMED EGGPLANT WITH SESAME, SCALLIONS, AND CHILI OIL

When it comes to vegetables, there are those who steam and those who boil (we're not talking about you fryers, grillers, or roasters right now), and I've always been a boiler. But recent encounters with some ardent steamers, and some steamy successes in the kitchen, have brought me around. Unlike boiling's bubbling jumble, steaming offers the structural advantage of keeping the food in place, so leeks don't get tangled, endive halves stay neat, and eggplant slices keep their shape. The seasoning that is inherent with salted boiling water is absent with steaming, so salt must be applied before or after.

The common collapsible metal steamer basket is fine for some things, but I like a bamboo steamer or a couscoussier because it allows the food to lie flat in a single layer.

Makes 6 servings

1 globe eggplant, or the equivalent amount of Italian, Japanese, Chinese, and so on

Salt

1 teaspoon sambal oelek—the chili paste available at Asian markets (I like the one in the little jar with a green top and gold label with a red rooster on it)

1 teaspoon sesame oil

2 tablespoons vegetable or olive oil

2 to 4 scallions, all the white and most of the green parts, thinly sliced

1 tablespoon sesame seeds, toasted (see page 9)

Peeling the eggplant is optional, but it is often nice to partly peel them, in stripes. If you're using a globe eggplant, cut it crosswise into ¾-inch slices. Other varieties can be cut lengthwise, to a similar thickness, in slices, halves, or quarters, depending on size. Sprinkle all sides with salt, about ¾ teaspoon, and let sit for 15 minutes. Get the steamer going, add the eggplant, and cook until very tender, about 15 minutes. Transfer the slices to a platter. Mix the sambal oelek with the oils and spoon it over the eggplant, sprinkle with scallions and sesame seeds, and serve warm or cool.

POTATO AND TOMATO GRATIN WITH BASIL

This dish manages, with elegance and ease, to combine the flavors of two of my childhood favorites—canned tomato soup and a bright orange cheesy dish that came from a package and had what I thought was the very unflattering name potatoes Og Rotten—and take them to another level.

Slicing potatoes for a gratin is often done on the mandoline, but if, like me, you are afraid of that little kitchen guillotine, you can use a knife. Cut a little slice off one side to make a flat spot for the potato to rest on, and go carefully. The slices might not be as perfect, but they'll be fine, and your fingers will remain whole. Waxy golden potatoes, like Yukon Gold or Yellow Finn, are the right ones for a gratin—they hold their shape and texture in a way that floury spuds like russets don't.

Makes 6 servings

3 ripe red baseball-size tomatoes

¾ cup cream, crème fraîche, or a combination, plus more as needed

¾ cup chicken stock (page 44), plus more as needed

1 garlic clove, pounded with a pinch of salt

Butter or oil for greasing the pan

1½ pounds waxy yellow potatoes

Salt

Leaves from 6 basil sprigs

Freshly ground black pepper

Bring a medium pot of water to a boil and drop in the tomatoes. Fish them out when the skins feel loose, around 30 seconds, and drop them into a bowl of ice water. With a paring knife, cut out the green stem ends, peel off the skins, and set the tomatoes aside.

In a small bowl, combine the cream, stock, and garlic paste and stir well.

Grease a 12 x 7-inch baking dish or a 9-inch cast-iron pan with butter or oil and heat the oven to 375°F.

Rinse the potatoes—they needn't be peeled unless the skins seem thick and tough. Start thinly slicing the potatoes about ⅛ inch thick and laying them in the dish, overlapping slightly, until you fill a single layer. Sprinkle with salt and a third of the basil leaves, torn into pieces. Spoon about a quarter of the cream mixture over, then thinly slice a tomato and arrange the slices over the potatoes. Sprinkle the tomato with salt and pepper and then keep slicing and layering until you have 4 layers of potato sandwiched with 3 of tomato. Make the top layer of potatoes nice and even so the gratin looks as good as it smells once baked. With your palms, press down

on the gratin—the liquid should just come up to your hands when you do. If not, add a little more cream or stock or both.

Cover with foil and bake for 30 minutes. Lift off the foil and press down on the gratin with a spatula to settle the layers. Re-cover and bake until a paring knife inserted into the middle of the gratin meets very little resistance, about 30 minutes. Uncover and continue baking until the top is very browned and bubbling, about 30 minutes. Let the gratin sit out of the oven for 5 minutes, then cut it into squares or rectangles and serve.

Fall

ROASTED CAULIFLOWER STRASCINATO WITH OLIVES AND CAPERS

I don't dress up in women's clothing, not often. I've been in drag twice, actually—strictly Halloween.

The first time, in Boston, where I was a notably tall college sophomore, it came to me in a flash that dressing as anything other than a fifties roller-waitress wouldn't do. Mostly I think I was intrigued with the stagecrafty gluing of burger, fries, and straw-stuck drink to the tray I planned to carry aloft with assurance and ease. What I'd given less thought to was that on roller skates, I looked seven feet tall. With my high socks, short skirt, cat-eye glasses, and wig, I was one scary waitress rolling at you.

Later, living in New York during the 1984 presidential campaign, I dressed as Walter Mondale's running mate, Geraldine Ferraro. We already had the same hairstyle, so I'd save on a wig, but my girlfriend didn't like my look and told me so. I probably should have taken off my skirt right then (it was her skirt actually), washed my face, and gone as someone else with poufy blond hair, but I didn't. A week later, Ronald Reagan won forty-nine out of fifty states in one of the biggest blowouts ever, and my girlfriend broke up with me.

Strascinato, turns out, doesn't mean "in drag," it means "dragged." So the cooked cauliflower is dragged not through eye shadow and blush, but in piquant tomato sauce, capers, and black olives. Which is kind of like puttanesca sauce, come to think of it, so maybe it does mean "in drag" after all.

The tomato puree can be made from canned tomatoes or the last of the summer crop roasted and passed through a food mill.

Makes 6 servings

1 cauliflower head, florets separated and cut into wedges

Cooking oil, olive or vegetable

Salt

2 garlic cloves, sliced or chopped

Crushed red pepper flakes

¾ cup tomato puree

¼ cup Niçoise olives, pitted and roughly chopped

2 tablespoons capers (salt-packed and very well soaked to desalinate, or brined capers rinsed well)

1 tablespoon chopped marjoram or oregano

1 tablespoon chopped parsley

Heat the oven to 450°F. Dress the cauliflower in a bowl with 2 tablespoons oil and ½ teaspoon salt and toss well to coat. Spread on a baking sheet and, when the oven is hot, roast until the cauliflower is browned and tender, 15 to 20 minutes.

Meanwhile, heat a skillet to medium-low and add 2 tablespoons oil and then the garlic and red pepper flakes. Stir until the garlic smells good, but don't let it brown at all, then add the tomato puree, olives, and capers. Stir and cook for 5 minutes or so, then turn the heat off and wait for the cauliflower to be done. When it is, add it and the herbs to the skillet, turn the heat to high, and stir well. Add a little water if needed to keep the mixture juicy, more oil if it needs shine. Taste, adjust, and eat it—hot, warm, or at room temperature.

* *Substitute wedges of fennel for the cauliflower.*
* *Consider adding chopped anchovies with the garlic.*

DAVIO'S BROCCOLI WITH GARLIC AND LEMON

My first restaurant job was as a parking valet at an Italian restaurant on New-bury Street in Boston. I would try to get glimpses of the food I was smelling as I ran through the kitchen, the keys to someone's Porsche or Mercedes jangling in my hand. Davio's was its unabashedly old-boy self with waiters standing tableside tossing Caesars, cooking Alfredo, and whipping zabaglione while the maître d' smiled and worked the twelve steps and the dishwasher sold cocaine that he kept in his shoe. Or so I was told. The cooks yelled and drank cold Miller High Life, floured flounder to fry with capers in dented sauté pans, baked cheesy pastas in monkey dishes, and splashed wine from plastic pour spouts to somehow pull off this wonderful garlic and lemon broccoli.

Makes 6 servings

1 big bunch broccoli (about 1 pound)

¼ cup olive oil

1 teaspoon salt

2 tablespoons butter

2 garlic cloves, chopped

Crushed red pepper flakes

½ cup white wine

Juice of ½ lemon

Cut the broccoli florets from the stalk and slice them ¼ inch thick. Peel the stalk and slice it similarly. Heat a skillet to high, add the oil and then the broc-coli, and stir as you sprinkle in the salt.

Cook over medium-high heat, stirring occasionally, to partly brown the broc-coli. After about 5 minutes, add ½ cup water and cover the skillet. Cook for 5 minutes (or a little less if you like crunchier broccoli—taste a piece and see) and then clear a little space in the center of the skillet. Add the butter and, when it has melted, the garlic and red pepper flakes. When the garlic smells good and has turned paler, but before it even hints at browning, stir everything up, raise the heat to high, and add the wine. Let the wine cook off for a minute, add the lemon juice, toss, taste, and serve hot.

PAN-FRIED POTATOES AL MATTONE

Boiled, flattened, and fried, these potatoes look—why, they look as if they've been struck with a blunt object! No, Colonel Mustard, it *wasn't* Professor Plum with the lead pipe in the conservatory. No, it was a brick! In the kitchen! Yes, and *I* did it! Hahahahaha! And I'd do it again! *Wahahahaha!*

Now let's eat. Where's Captain Catsup? (Answer: page 253.)

Makes 6 servings

12 Ping-Pong-ball-size waxy yellow potatoes (about 1¼ pounds—Yukon Gold, Yellow Finn, Bintje, German Butterball, and so on)

Salt

Oil for frying

Put the potatoes in a pot, cover them with water by ½ inch, and add 1 teaspoon salt. Bring them to a boil, lower the heat to a simmer, and cook until they are tender all the way through, about 20 minutes.

Drain the potatoes and let them cool for at least 30 minutes. Heat the oven to warm for holding batches as they are fried. Using a spatula or some other handy flat utensil (saucer, small saucepan, clean brick . . .), press down on the potatoes one by one to flatten them. Crush them just enough to split the skins and splay them out a bit—be careful not to break them to pieces.

Heat a skillet to medium and add oil to a depth of ¼ inch or so, then as many of the crushed potatoes as will fit in a single layer. Fry until the potatoes are golden brown and crispy around the edges, adjusting the heat as needed. Turn them and brown the other sides, sprinkle them with salt when done, and keep them warm in the oven while you fry the next batch.

* *Use rendered duck fat left over from confit (page 117) to fry in.*

ROASTED WINTER SQUASH WITH BROWN BUTTER

Meaty, thick-walled winter squashes that cook up dry are best for puree and for ravioli filling. The juicier types are more suited to soup-making. For this recipe, I like Buttercup and other kabocha types, butternut, or Honeynut.

Makes 6 servings

1 hard winter squash (about 2 pounds)

½ teaspoon salt

Good olive oil

3 tablespoons butter

12 sage leaves, roughly chopped (optional)

Heat the oven to 450°F. Carefully cut the squash in half from top to bottom and scoop out the seeds and stringy stuff. Season the cut sides with salt and rub them with oil. Place them cut side up on a baking sheet, cover them loosely with foil, and roast until they are very soft, about 45 minutes to an hour. Times will vary with squash size and variety, so test for doneness by inserting a paring knife blade—it should meet with no resistance.

When the squash pieces are cool enough to handle, use a large spoon to scoop the flesh out. Crank it through a food mill, spin it in the food processor, or stir it vigorously with a whisk to puree. Put the butter in a small saucepan or skillet and heat it on high. When it has melted, the butter will foam and then begin to brown. Wait until it is colored around the edges and smelling nutty, then add the sage leaves, if you're using them, and quickly pour the butter into the squash puree. Stir well, taste, adjust, and serve hot.

* *Eat this as a nest for a poached egg with a spoonful of harissa sauce (page 261), and you will not regret it.*

CREAMY KALE WITH ONIONS

Before lacinato kale spread like kudzu across every restaurant menu, we cooked it all the time. We listed it as cavolo nero on menus, because lacinato kale sounded less appealing and would go, we thought, unordered. We were wrong there, but the Italian, if misspelled slightly—*cavallo nero*—does seem to fit what lacinato kale has become: a dark horse vegetable. The appeal of shredding it raw and trendily serving it as a salad eludes me yet, but I do love it in soups and stews, with anchovies on toasts, and in this simple creamy dish that seems to allow for a nuance that the massaged and aggressively dressed salad treatment does not.

Makes 6 servings

3 tablespoons cooking oil, olive or vegetable

1 yellow onion, diced

Crushed red pepper flakes

Salt

1 big bunch lacinato kale, leaves stripped from stems, washed, drained (not spun), and torn

½ cup cream

½ teaspoon red wine vinegar or lemon juice

Heat a skillet to high and add the oil and then the onion, red pepper flakes, and ½ teaspoon salt. Stir until it gets going, then turn to medium and cook, stirring occasionally, until the onion is soft and very lightly browned, 15 to 20 minutes. Use a lid or a splash of water if it colors too much before getting soft. Add the kale, ¼ teaspoon salt, and ¼ cup water. Cover and cook, stirring occasionally and adding splashes of water if it gets at all sizzly, until the kale is very tender, about 20 minutes. Uncover, add the cream and vinegar or lemon juice, and cook for a few minutes more. The kale should be saucy but not soupy. Taste, adjust, and serve now or reheat, with a splash of water, when ready.

Winter

RUTABAGA SLAW

Midwinter, crisp raw root vegetable slaw can be just the crunchy thing to add a picnicky feel to grilled and sliced meat or fried fish or chicken. It's nice tucked into a ham sandwich as well.

Makes 6 servings

2 baseball-size rutabagas, peeled

1 large carrot

¾ teaspoon salt

2 teaspoons white wine vinegar

¼ cup crème fraîche (page 248) or mayonnaise (page 264)

2 teaspoons Dijon mustard

Freshly ground black pepper

Grate the rutabagas and carrot on the large holes of a grater, angling them so that you get the longest possible shreds. In a mixing bowl, toss the rutabagas and carrot with the salt and vinegar, and let sit for 10 minutes. Tip off any liquid that has drained out of the roots, add the remaining ingredients, and mix well. Taste, adjust, and eat right away, or wait—it only gets better and will keep, refrigerated, for a couple of days.

* *Just before serving, mix in finely chopped chives, tarragon, chervil, or parsley.*
* *Replace the vinegar with lime juice, the mustard with chopped jalapeños, black pepper with toasted cumin seeds, and add chopped cilantro. Tacos?*
* *Fishcakes (page 159)?*

STEAMED AND GRILLED BELGIAN ENDIVES

This simple recipe surprises people every time, even Alice; I remember her commenting on it once at Chez Panisse, saying it was the best *fennel* she ever had, and that we should always cook it that way. No one disagreed.

Makes 6 servings

3 Belgian endive heads

Salt

1 teaspoon sweet white wine, such as Moscato, or dry wine with ½ teaspoon sugar dissolved in it

Cooking oil, olive or vegetable

Cut the Belgian endives in half lengthwise and trim away any brown parts. Sprinkle with ½ teaspoon salt and set aside to absorb for 5 minutes. Steam until the endives are completely tender, but not mushy, 20 to 30 minutes. Test for doneness by inserting a paring knife blade—it should meet with very little resistance. Let the endives cool for a few minutes (or hours) and brush them with the wine and then some oil. Sprinkle on a bit more salt, then grill the endives over hot coals to mark well and heat through.

* *Perfect to grill with and serve alongside meat or fish, with a couple spoonfuls of fried herb salsa (page 250).*
* *If a hot grill is not in the plan for tonight, you can brown the steamed endives in a cast-iron pan or under the broiler.*

BELGIAN ENDIVE GRATIN WITH PECORINO AND PROSCIUTTO

This is a dish for when "simply steamed" sounds less good than "browned, bubbly, and baked with cream, ham, and cheese."

Makes 6 servings

4 Belgian endive heads

Salt

Cooking oil, olive or vegetable

1 large yellow onion, thinly sliced

2 or 3 slices prosciutto

2 tablespoons chopped thyme leaves

3 tablespoons butter

¼ cup white wine

½ cup heavy cream

Scant ¼ cup grated pecorino or Parmesan

Cut the Belgian endives in half lengthwise and trim away any brown parts. Sprinkle with ½ teaspoon salt and set aside to absorb.

Heat a skillet to high and add 3 tablespoons oil, then the onion and ¼ teaspoon salt. Stir until it gets going, then turn to medium and cook, stirring occasionally, until soft and very lightly browned, 15 to 20 minutes. Use a lid or a splash of water if the onion colors too much before getting soft. Tear the prosciutto slices into the skillet—cutting with a knife makes prosciutto slices stick frustratingly together. Add the thyme, stir, and let sizzle for a minute. Stir in ⅓ cup water.

Spread the onion mixture into a baking dish that will snugly fit the Belgian endive halves in a single layer. Heat the oven to 400°F.

Rinse or wipe out the skillet and return it to medium-high heat. Add 1 tablespoon oil and 2 tablespoons butter to the skillet and, when the mixture stops foaming, the Belgian endives with the cut side down. If they don't all fit, then do the browning in two batches. As the endives become nicely browned, set them atop the onion, cut side up—no need to brown the other side. When they are all in the dish, pour the wine and cream over them, dot them with the remaining butter, and bake, uncovered, until a paring knife blade inserted into the middle meets very little resistance, about 25 minutes. Sprinkle the pecorino over the endives and bake 8 to 10 minutes more, or until they're all browned and bubbly. Serve hot.

* *Substitute sage or rosemary for the thyme, pancetta or bacon for the prosciutto.*
* *Serve with poached eggs and toast, roasted or grilled meats or poultry, and a green salad to contrast with the richness.*

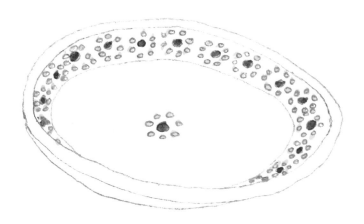

FRIED PARSNIP CHIPS

I shave parsnips into long sinuous strips for frying using nothing more complicated than a Y-shaped vegetable peeler and a fork. Many have more mechanized devices for this sort of thing, and I acknowledge their bravery and innovative spirit, but here's what I do:

Peel a parsnip and then stab the tines of a table fork into the fat end. With a peeler, take strips from the parsnip, holding it in place with the fork and peeling toward you from thin end to thick. Arriving at the often fibrous core, turn the parsnip and whittle down the next side and then the next until you can't get any more. Parsnips will not discolor like potatoes, so no need to put the strips in water.

Fill a deep skillet or saucepan with frying oil to a depth of at least 3 inches. Heat the oil to 325°F, or until a parsnip chip slipped in sinks but resurfaces quickly and bubbles there cheerfully. Add a handful of chips to the oil—you can crowd them a bit, as they will soon shrink and make room—and poke with a spider to untangle them. Fry until the chips have just stopped bubbling and are lightly browned. Drain them on paper or a wire rack and sprinkle them with salt—don't despair if they seem leathery at first; they will crisp as they cool a little.

By now you know that they are good for snacking on. Serve them also next to slices of roasted or grilled meat or poultry, or fried or baked fish. Nice and crunchy sprinkled over winter salads of arugula, escarole, or radicchio.

* Parsnip-frying oil can be strained and saved, refrigerated, for reuse for up to a week.

SWEET AND HOT SAVOY CABBAGE

This simple, satisfying recipe is inspired by one from Cecilia Chiang, the incomparable doyenne of Chinese cooking in America. When her masterful cookbook *The Seventh Daughter* came out, we celebrated with a feast at Chez Panisse that was at once Chinese, Californian, and wine friendly. It was such a hit, and so much fun to cook, that we have repeated it every year to mark the lunar New Year and to introduce diners to an elegant kind of Chinese cookery that fits perfectly in our fresh, produce-driven kitchens. Cecilia herself often comes for dinner, which is both delightful and terrifying, and, at ninety-something, she continues to charm and amaze us with her wisdom, generosity, and youthful wide smile.

Makes at least 6 servings

1 savoy cabbage, 2 to 3 pounds (or green, or napa)

Salt

6 tablespoons cooking oil, olive or vegetable

Crushed red pepper flakes

Sugar

Rice vinegar (or champagne, white wine, or cider vinegar)

Split the cabbage in half through the core. Cut the halves into thirds so you have 6 wedges. Slice each across into ½-inch strips, stopping when you reach the core. Put the cabbage in a colander, sprinkle it with 1 tablespoon salt, toss, and let it sit for 30 minutes to wilt and drain a bit.

Heat a skillet to high and add 3 tablespoons of the oil, then half the cabbage. Stir, toss, and cook for 4 minutes, then add red pepper flakes, 1 tablespoon sugar, 2 tablespoons vinegar, and 2 tablespoons water. Stir, toss, and cook until the cabbage is tender but with bite, an additional minute or two. Taste, adjust, and tip out into a bowl while you repeat with the remaining cabbage. Really good right away and even better after a few hours or, refrigerated, a couple days.

WHITE ROOT PUREE
(WHICH IS VERY GOOD WITH BLACK TRUFFLE...
ALSO WITHOUT)

That black truffles go so well with white food seems so black-and-white obvious that it couldn't possibly bear out, but it does. White foods do tend toward the mild, flavorwise, and so are just the stage for pungent, yet often elusive, black truffles to sing out from. Happily, even without them, this smooth puree still purrs luxury.

Makes 6 servings

1 pound large white turnips
Salt
1 pound parsnips
1 pound potatoes

½ cup half-and-half, more as desired
6 tablespoons unsalted butter

Peel the turnips and cut them into ½-inch-thick slices. Sprinkle them with ¼ teaspoon salt. Do the same thing with the parsnips, but don't mix the two vegetables together, as they may not cook at the same rate. Set the turnips and parsnips in separate parts of a steamer and steam until very tender—cut and taste a piece of each to be sure.

Meanwhile, peel the potatoes and cut them into quarters: large chunks absorb less water and yield a richer, more flavorful mash. Rinse and cover them with cold water in a saucepan. Add 1 teaspoon salt, bring them to a boil over high heat, and lower the heat to a simmer. Cook until the potatoes are completely tender but not falling apart, about 20 minutes. To be sure they are ready, take a piece out of the pot and cut it at the thickest spot. It should sort of break apart and look dry inside. Tasting a slice will confirm doneness and give you a sense of seasoning. Drain the potatoes and let them sit in the colander to release steam for a few minutes. Put the pan back on very low heat and add the half-and-half. Set a food mill over the pan and begin passing the potatoes, parsnips, and turnips through, adding chunks of butter as you go. Stir the puree to mix completely, then taste and adjust with more butter or salt for flavor, half-and-half for texture.

Reheat if cooled, but slowly and carefully with plenty of gentle, thorough stirring—purees can stick and scorch.

* *Add as much grated black truffle as you can afford to the final puree.*
* *Replace the parsnips or turnips with celery root or rutabagas.*

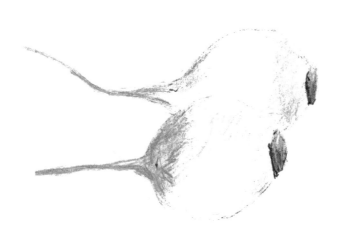

SAUCES

I remember my brother teasing me, when we were boys, about making my own special sauce for the frozen burger patties that would spit grease and hunch into domes as we pan-fried them and toasted English muffins for buns. It was early days of sauce-making for me, and I, like so many others, was doing crude things with ketchup and mayonnaise, squirting one into the other and stirring in pickle relish, shaking in Tabasco, considering Worcestershire. Sweet, simple, and splashy. If cooking were swimming, special sauce would be a cannonball—it gets attention at first, but soon becomes silly and brash, an invitation, as if one were needed, for a big brother's mockery. Later, seeking more sympathetic notice, one develops a more sophisticated repertoire.

There is still a place for some splash and sting in sauces like fiery harissa and nutty romesco, but also headfirst dives that display daring and commitment while being quieter and more soigné, like tart, elegant vinaigrette or rich beurre blanc, a pale, pretty sauce that pools at the fins of fish with a no-splash sort of confidence.

RED WINE VINAIGRETTE

My go-to basic dressing, especially for salads of little lettuces, arugula, or watercress, and one that can be adapted in many ways with additions of shallots, fresh herbs, lemon, different vinegars, cream, egg yolk . . .

Makes ¼ cup

1 small garlic clove, or ½ clove, either pounded with salt or simply cracked once with the side of a knife

⅛ teaspoon salt

Black pepper

2 teaspoons red wine vinegar

½ teaspoon Dijon mustard, or more, or none, or whole grain

3 tablespoons good olive oil

Mix the garlic, salt, pepper, vinegar, and mustard in a small bowl or jar with a lid. Stir the oil into the bowl or add to the jar and shake. Shake or seriously stir the vinaigrette again to blend completely just before dressing the salad. If you used a whole, cracked garlic clove, take it out after 10 minutes or up to a couple of hours and discard it or the flavor will get too strong.

PINK PEPPERCORN AND GRAPEFRUIT VINAIGRETTE

Pink peppercorns grow on trees all over Berkeley, and when I put them on the menu, I harvest them on my way in to work. The trees are beautiful, with spiky-leaved branches drooping down like willows and bunches of peppercorns hanging like tiny pink gumballs. But chew into one and you'll get a hot bite more mind- than bubble-blowing. Though unrelated, pink is spicy like black, but in a resinous, piney way. We use it in small doses, ground up to mix with shallots and zest in the winter and to splash over salads of sliced grapefruit or orange, and avocado or thin slices of raw fish. This dressing may be too fierce for delicate lettuces, but tender mustard greens, mizuna, and frisée can take it.

Makes ¼ cup

1 shallot, finely diced

¼ teaspoon salt

1 teaspoon grated grapefruit zest

1 tablespoon grapefruit juice

1 teaspoon lemon juice

1 teaspoon red wine vinegar

1 teaspoon ground pink peppercorns

3 tablespoons good olive oil

Mix everything but the oil and let it marinate for a few minutes. Add the oil, taste, adjust—it may need more oil if the grapefruit juice is very sour—and get zesty pink on:

* *Salad of avocado and radishes or grapefruit slices and something green such as arugula or cress.*
* *Raw slices of the freshest fish (page 24).*
* *Whipped ricotta or creamy mozzarella and roasted golden beets (page 62).*

TOMATO VINAIGRETTE

I like this summer-only sauce because you can really sling it around—it's like a little gazpachito that you can splash over mozzarella or ricotta, on grilled fish, or use to dress panzanella or any other salad of the season.

Makes 1½ to 2 cups

1 small garlic clove, pounded with ¼ teaspoon salt

Freshly ground black pepper

2 teaspoons red wine vinegar

1 shallot, finely diced, or 2 scallions, all the white and most of the green parts, thinly sliced

2 ripe tomatoes or 1 pint basket cherry tomatoes

3 tablespoons good olive oil

Salt

1 loose cup basil, mint, or cilantro leaves, or 1 tablespoon chopped marjoram or oregano

1 tablespoon chopped parsley

Mix the garlic paste, pepper, vinegar, and shallot together in a medium mixing bowl. Let the shallot marinate for a few minutes and then cut one of the tomatoes in half at the equator, gently squeeze the seeds out, and grate it into the bowl. Start on the cut side and grate right down until all you have left is the skin—it won't go through the holes, so you can really push it. If the tomato is big, you may not need to grate the whole half. You want about ⅓ cup pulpy juice. If you're using cherry tomatoes, pulse a handful in the food processor to break them up a little, or halve them with a knife, then pass them through a food mill to get rid of the skins before adding them to the shallot mixture. Stir in the oil. Dice the remaining large tomatoes, or cut the cherry tomatoes into halves, sprinkle them with salt, and add them to the bowl, stirring in the herbs.

* *Sauce for fish fillets stuffed with bread crumbs, saffron, pine nuts, and currants (page 149), or pan-fried fishcakes (page 159).*

WALNUT VINAIGRETTE

Makes ⅓ cup

1 shallot, finely diced

¼ teaspoon salt

1 teaspoon red wine vinegar

1 teaspoon sherry vinegar

2 tablespoons toasted walnuts (see page 9)

¼ cup good olive oil

Mix the shallot, salt, and vinegars together in a small bowl and let marinate for a few minutes.

Crush the walnuts nearly to a paste in a mortar or with the side of a chef's knife, add them to the shallot-vinegar mixture, and stir in the oil. Taste and adjust.

* *Replace the walnuts with hazelnuts, pecans, or almonds.*
* *Dress Belgian endives (page 133) or other hearty greens.*

CITRUS ZEST VINAIGRETTE

Makes ¼ cup

1 teaspoon grated zest: lemon, orange, lime, grapefruit . . .

1 tablespoon minced shallot

¼ teaspoon salt

2 teaspoons lemon juice (or a combination of citrus juices)

1 teaspoon red wine vinegar

Freshly ground black pepper

3 tablespoons good olive oil

The citrus zest has to be in very tiny pieces for this dressing, and there are a couple of ways to accomplish this. One is to use a vegetable peeler to cut strips of skin from the fruit, line up the strips, and cut them into little sticks, then line up the sticks and cut them into tiny bits. Another is to use the smallest holes on the box grater and then go over the gratings with a knife. Or, if you must, use the Microplane (which, by my lights, creates too feathery an effect—I like little bits, not micro bits). Mix the shallot, salt, citrus juice, vinegar, and black pepper with the zest and let sit for 5 minutes to marinate the shallot. Stir in the oil.

* *For dressing salads of sliced citrus (page 126), avocados, or beets, and to spoon over baked or grilled fish.*

BÉARNAISE

One of the things I love about béarnaise sauce is how it is both fluffy, buttery feminine and beefy, clubby masculine at the same time, like a weight-lifting stockbroker in French drag. Maybe béarnaise is best known on slices of beef, but lamb, asparagus, and fried potatoes look glamorous under its golden veil as well.

Makes 6 servings, about 1 rich and generous cup

1 tablespoon plus 1 teaspoon tarragon leaves

½ cup white wine

¼ cup white wine vinegar

Freshly ground black pepper

2 egg yolks

¼ teaspoon salt

1½ sticks unsalted butter, melted, warm, not hot

½ lemon

Chop 1 tablespoon tarragon leaves and put them, the wine, vinegar, and plenty of black pepper in a medium saucepan. Bring the mixture to a boil over high heat, lower to a fast simmer, and cook until it is reduced to about 2 tablespoons. Pour the reduction into a medium mixing bowl and let it cool for a few minutes.

In a small saucepan, bring an inch or so of water to a simmer. Keeping the heat low, set the bowl over the pan, add the egg yolks and ¼ teaspoon salt, and start whisking. You want the yolks to be just warm lest they curdle, so move the bowl away from the heat if it starts getting hot. Continue whisking and maintaining warmth until the yolks have turned paler and thickened enough that they leave streaks where the bottom of the bowl is visible for a moment. Begin slowly whisking in the warm melted butter, just a tablespoon at a time at first, and gradually increasing to a steady stream. When the butter is all in, the béarnaise can be thinned, if needed, with a spoonful of warm water.

Finely chop the remaining tarragon leaves and whisk them, the salt, and a squeeze of lemon juice into the sauce. Taste and adjust and keep warm, not hot, until ready to serve. If the béarnaise breaks, a spin in the blender will usually fix it. If it cools, reheat it carefully, whisking, over steam.

BEURRE BLANC

The acidity needs to be a little high in this buttery sauce, or it can seem like just a lot of butter . . . which, admittedly, it is, but a considered quantity of creamy beurre blanc can transform a plate of simply baked fish and boiled vegetables into something elegant and special. Soft herbs—chervil, chives, tarragon, basil, or parsley—are good to chop and sprinkle or blend smooth and stir in.

Makes 1 decadent yet delicate cup

2 shallots, diced tiny

2 thyme sprigs

1 cup white wine

2 tablespoons champagne or white wine vinegar

Freshly ground black pepper

2 tablespoons heavy cream

1½ sticks unsalted butter

½ teaspoon salt

½ lemon

Combine the shallots, thyme, wine, vinegar, and a couple cranks of black pepper in a small saucepan and bring the mixture to a boil over high heat. Lower the heat and simmer until reduced to a thin syrup, about 2 tablespoons. Remove the thyme sprigs, add the cream, and when it bubbles, begin to add the butter, whisking a couple of pieces into the gently simmering reduction. When they melt and become creamy, add a couple more pieces, whisking away and regulating the heat by changing the flame/setting, but also by adding more butter. When it's all in, add the salt and squeeze in the lemon juice. The sauce will be smooth and pale, and should feel quite warm and stay that way in a warm spot near the oven or in a double boiler until you're ready to use it.

* *Splash a little of your vegetable-cooking water or fish-cooking juices onto the plate for the sauce to mingle with so that it remains rich, but not too.*
* *Make an herb puree to stir into the finished sauce: Pick leaves off the stems of chervil, basil, or parsley to make a loose ½ cup. Add a spoonful of tarragon leaves to the parsley, if you like, and puree the herbs with 1 tablespoon cream, a pinch of salt, and just enough warm water to make it work in your blender or food processor. Whisk into the beurre blanc.*

CRÈME FRAÎCHE, WITH VARIATIONS

Made of cream but somehow lighter than cream, crème fraîche makes itself overnight, and like its leaner, sourer cousin yogurt, it can be flavored with a free hand, mixing in chopped or pounded herbs, toasted and crushed spices, citrus zests and juices.

Start the next batch when the current one is running low, and you'll never run out!

Makes about 2 cups

2 cups heavy cream
2 tablespoons buttermilk or crème fraîche

In a small bowl, stir to mix completely, then leave at room temperature, covered, overnight. If it seems not thick enough, you can leave it another night. Refrigerate once thickened.

Horseradish Crème Fraîche

For ¼ cup crème fraîche, put 1 tablespoon freshly grated horseradish in a small bowl and add 1 teaspoon champagne vinegar or white wine vinegar and a pinch of salt. Stir, then add the mixture to the crème fraîche. Grind in some black pepper if you like. Taste and add more horseradish if you like it spicier.

* *Sauce braised beef (like the short ribs, page 189) or chicken, sandwiches, hot dogs, or hamburgers.*
* *Dressing to spoon over sliced beets or for potato salad.*

Herb Crème Fraîche

For ¼ cup crème fraîche, chop and pound 1 loose cup basil, mint, chervil, or cilantro leaves. Stir them into the crème fraîche with a sprinkle of salt and the juice of ½ lime or lemon. Add a little pounded garlic if you like. Or, instead of the pounded herbs, use 1 tablespoon thinly sliced chives and a teaspoon finely chopped tarragon.

* *Dressing for leafy salads like romaine, green and red leaf, and butter lettuces. Also good for dressing coleslaw or other thinly sliced vegetables like carrots, turnips, rutabaga, and fennel.*
* *Dressing to spoon over salads of raw vegetables, like cucumbers and tomatoes, or cooked vegetables, like asparagus and beets.*
* *Filling for an omelet or spooned over scrambled eggs.*
* *Dip for your chip.*

Saffron and Lime Crème Fraîche

For ¼ cup crème fraîche, crush ¼ teaspoon saffron threads in a cup or small bowl. Squeeze in the juice of ½ lime and a pinch of salt. Stir to dissolve the saffron, then stir into the crème fraîche.

* *Sauce for grilled, baked, or fried fish, shrimp or scallops, or grilled or roasted lamb or chicken.*
* *Garnish, along with a little chopped mint, basil, or cilantro, for vegetable soups, especially tomato or cauliflower.*
* *Dressing to spoon over salads of raw vegetables, like cucumbers and tomatoes, or over cooked vegetables, like asparagus and Belgian endives.*

FRIED HERB SALSA

When a simple parsley and garlic salsa verde needs a little flair to help it get noticed among, say, smoky grilled meats, you can add powerful sage, savory, and rosemary, very finely chopped and very sparingly. Frying herb leaves before mixing them in allows them to be their whole spiky selves, adding a polite thorniness, giving sweet parsley a kind, crunchy kick.

Makes 1 cup

1 garlic clove, pounded with a pinch of salt

⅓ cup finely chopped parsley

⅓ cup good olive oil

⅓ cup crumbled fried herbs (recipe follows)

Mix everything together, stir, taste, adjust, and spoon all over, especially on cast-iron pan roast (page 186), chicken al mattone (page 163), braised short ribs (page 189), grilled vegetables, beans, toast even.

Fried Herbs

If you find yourself buying whole bunches of herbs like sage or rosemary when you really just need a sprig or two, and if you feel bad that the rest of the bunch tends to molder and mock every time you open the fridge, I have the solution: fry! Why? Because, though it takes a bit of oil and effort, herbs fried crispy are tempered in flavor, crunchy of texture, and live a longer and more useful life.

Cooking oil, vegetable or olive

Leaves from 1 bunch rosemary, sage, or savory, patted dry if necessary to avoid oil spits and splatters

Salt

In a small saucepan or skillet, pour enough oil for the herbs, fried in a few batches, to swim around in, at least ¾ inch. The oil won't really be reusable for anything else, unfortunately, since frying herbs makes it bitter, so I try not to use too much. Heat the oil to 325°F or until it is shimmery, not smoking, and a leaf dropped in sizzles enthusiastically, but does not scare you out of the kitchen. Fry a batch of herb leaves, and when the sizzling has nearly stopped, dip them out and onto paper to drain while you fry the next batch. Sprinkle them with salt and use them right away or refrigerate them, covered tightly; they'll last at least a week.

* *Extra fried herbs can be sprinkled over roasted, grilled, or braised meats; crumbled and tossed with boiled or roasted vegetables, or sprinkled over fried ones; floated on bowls of soup; mixed with fresh garlic and parsley for more salsa!*

* _____ *(fill in the blank)*

* _____ *(with your variation)*

ROMESCO SAUCE

The sauce served at a true calçotada is just for onions and is not even romesco exactly, but really, this sauce is good with so many things. When we make a batch at Chez Panisse, enthusiasts declare, and prove, their ability to eat a quantity of it with nothing other than a spoon.

Makes enough for now and later (which you'll want)

¼ cup sweet chili powder (about 8 whole chilies or a scant 2 ounces; see harissa, page 261, for more on this)

½ cup toasted and finely ground hazelnuts (page 9)

½ cup toasted and finely ground almonds

1 or 2 garlic cloves, pounded with a pinch of salt

1 cup toasted bread crumbs (page 79)

1 cup good olive oil

1 tablespoon red wine vinegar

Juice of ½ orange

Put the chili powder in a medium bowl, add ⅜ cup boiling water, and set it aside for 30 minutes to hydrate. Stir in the remaining ingredients and cut the other half of the orange into wedges and give them to the kids. The romesco should be crumbly and oily, while the kids will be sticky and happy. Taste the sauce and add more garlic, oil, vinegar, or salt as needed.

* *Romesco is not unappreciated on halved hard-boiled eggs or grilled fish or squid, or stirred into a bowl of warm chickpeas or, especially even, a bowl of fish soup (page 153). You can also put the whole business in a blender with a little water and whiz it smooth, almost like mayonnaise, to serve with shrimp cooked any way.*

SALSA ROSSA

This, to me, is a winter sauce, to be made with preserved tomatoes. In summer, when tomatoes are ripe and sweet, there are better things to do with them. Salsa rossa may be reminiscent of a more familiar sauce, which I won't name, but will tell a story about.

The Tomato family went for a walk and little Tomato was lagging behind. Father Tomato went over to him and stepped on him and said, "Catch up!"

Makes about 2½ cups and freezes well

¼ cup olive or vegetable oil

1 yellow onion, thinly sliced

1 small carrot, thinly sliced

1 celery stalk, thinly sliced

½ teaspoon salt

Crushed red pepper flakes

1 teaspoon fennel seeds, toasted and finely ground (see page 9)

1 teaspoon coriander seeds, toasted and finely ground

3 allspice berries, toasted and finely ground

3 whole cloves, toasted and finely ground

14.5-ounce can whole peeled tomatoes, roughly chopped, juices included

1 tablespoon brown sugar, lightly packed (optional)

1 tablespoon red wine vinegar

Heat a medium saucepan to high. Add the oil and then the onion, carrot, celery, and salt. Stir, lower the heat, and cover the pan. Check and stir after a few minutes. Lower the heat and splash in a little water if there is any browning going on. Cook until very tender, about 15 minutes. Add the remaining ingredients, raise the heat, and, stirring frequently, bring to a simmer. Lower the heat to just barely bubbling and cook, stirring occasionally, for 30 minutes. Puree in a food mill, blender, or food processor. Gets better in the fridge and will last, covered, for at least a week.

* *Classic with boiled meats or poultry. Just as good with braises and grilled meats, especially pork or duck. Tasty with fried things, like . . . potatoes?*
* *Goes wherever that other red sauce goes and can get into fancier places as well.*

BÉCHAMEL

This béchamel sauce is on the thin side, ideal for 15-Layer Lasagna (page 144).

Makes about 3¼ cups

3 cups milk

4½ tablespoons butter

3 tablespoons plus 1 teaspoon all-purpose flour

¼ teaspoon salt

In a small saucepan, heat the milk to just below boiling.

In a separate small saucepan, melt the butter over very low heat. Add the flour and stir with a whisk for 3 minutes. Raise the heat to medium and add a little hot milk, about ¼ cup, whisking constantly. Whisk until the milk is completely mixed in, then add another dose of milk and whisk to a smooth consistency again. Repeat, whisking all the while, always waiting to add more milk until the previous addition is fully incorporated. Raise the heat to medium-high halfway through the milk additions. When the sauce has the thickness of heavy cream, whisk in all the remaining milk and the salt. Switch from the whisk to a wooden spoon, or a rubber spatula, and continue stirring, being sure to cover every spot of the bottom of the pan to prevent scorching. Stir until the béchamel just begins to simmer, then turn the heat to the lowest setting—you may need to use a flame diffuser if your burner won't go very low. Stir a minute more, cover the pot incompletely, and continue to cook, stirring occasionally, for 10 minutes. Pass the béchamel through a strainer to remove any lumps.

* *For macaroni and cheese sauce, add cheese—a lot, and this is a good time to grate up all the not-moldy ends that are kicking around your fridge. If you're adding cheese, allow the béchamel to cool for 5 minutes or so first, or it may curdle. If it does, a (careful) spin in the blender will fix it easily.*
* *Dress boiled vegetables with béchamel and bake them in a casserole dish for a creamy gratin. Finish with cheese or toasted bread crumbs (page 79) on top.*

CILANTRO-COCONUT CHUTNEY

This is one of those chunky sauces that seem to go with nearly everything or, like romesco, with nothing: I've seen them both eaten straight. From a spoon . . . okay, by me.

Makes 1 cup of the tropics

½ cup unsweetened dried shredded coconut

1 cup roughly chopped cilantro leaves and stems (about ½ bunch)

1 garlic clove, pounded with a pinch of salt

2 teaspoons grated ginger (about 1 inch)

½ teaspoon sugar

¼ teaspoon salt

¼ cup olive or vegetable oil

1 lime

1 jalapeño, seeded and diced (or more or less)

Heat the oven to 300°F. Spread the coconut on a baking sheet and toast until it is lightly browned, about 4 minutes. Set a timer because coconut burns easily. Set it aside to cool.

In a blender, combine the cilantro, garlic paste, ginger, sugar, salt, oil, the juice of the lime, and ¼ cup cold water. Spin until the mixture is nearly smooth, but still has some bits. Pour it into a bowl, add the jalapeño and toasted coconut, mix well, taste, and adjust. Add more oil or water if needed for flow.

* *Serve with vegetable (page 27) or fish fritters (page 28), with lamb or eggs, or mixed into rice.*

CAPONATINA

Savory and sweet, eggplant caponata is one of the gems of Sicily. Like ratatouille, caponata made with ripe eggplant and tomatoes seems to wrap up summer like a time capsule of the season.

But caponata doesn't have to end with summer. I've started making it with fennel, artichokes, celery, or hard squashes. In their inspiring book *Sicilian Home Cooking: Family Recipes from Gangivecchio*, Wanda and Giovanna Tornabene have a recipe for a delicious all-greens version that can be made year-round.

We eat this like the salad it's meant to be, alongside a spoonful of ricotta, a slice of mozzarella, or half a hard-boiled egg, but I also like to chop everything smaller, use it as a relish-y sauce on meats or fish, and call it, fondly, caponatina.

Makes enough for leftovers that get better in the refrigerator for at least a week

1 large eggplant or a few smaller ones (about 1¼ pounds), cut into ½-inch dice

Salt

Cooking oil, olive or vegetable

1 yellow onion, diced

1 red or orange pepper, diced

1 cup thinly sliced celery (about 2 stalks)

1 ripe red tomato

2 garlic cloves, thinly sliced

Crushed red pepper flakes

Leaves from 5 mint sprigs (about ½ cup)

1 tablespoon sugar

2 teaspoons red wine vinegar

½ cup pitted and roughly chopped green olives (Picholine, Lucques, or Castelvetrano)

2 tablespoons capers (salt-packed and very well soaked to desalinate, or brined capers rinsed well)

Good olive oil

Put the eggplant in a mixing bowl and sprinkle it with 1 teaspoon salt. Heat a skillet to medium-high and add 3 tablespoons cooking oil and half the eggplant. Shake to settle and leave it to get browned for about 4 minutes. Stir the eggplant around and leave it to brown some more. When it is looking nicely colored and feeling tender, 8 to 10 minutes total, set it aside and cook the rest of the eggplant in 3 more tablespoons cooking oil. Set the eggplant aside, wipe out the skillet, and return it to high heat.

Add ¼ cup cooking oil and then the onion, red pepper, and ½ teaspoon salt. Stir until things get going, then reduce the heat to medium-low, add the celery, and cook, stirring occasionally, until the vegetables are just getting tender, about 10 minutes.

Meanwhile, cut the tomato in half along the equator and gently squeeze out the seeds. Using the large holes of a box grater, grate the halves, on the cut side, into a bowl. Grate right down until all you have left is the skin—it won't go through the holes, so you can really push it. Discard the skin and set the pulp aside.

Move the onion, pepper, and celery to the edges of the skillet, add a little more cooking oil if it looks dry, and put the garlic and red pepper flakes in the middle. Let them sizzle there until the garlic smells really good but isn't browning at all, tear up the mint, and add it to the skillet and stir for 10 seconds. Add the sugar, vinegar, olives, capers, eggplant, grated tomato, and ½ cup water and stir while you raise the heat and bring the mixture to a simmer. Lower it to a murmur and cook for 10 minutes, stirring occasionally. Let the caponatina cool, stir in a tablespoon or two of olive oil, taste, and adjust.

CHERMOULA

Though it can be made with additions of mint and parsley, chermoula is amazingly good with just cilantro.

Makes 1 verdant cup

1 bunch cilantro

1 garlic clove, pounded with a pinch of salt

¾ cup good olive oil

¼ teaspoon salt

Roughly chop the cilantro, stems and all (excluding any yellowed parts), and put it in the blender with the garlic paste, oil, and salt. Pulse and then puree till smooth.

* *Spoon over couscous (page 141), chickpeas, beans, or eggs.*

HARISSA

Mild chilies are great for making harissa sauce. I like Hatch, Joe Parker, Anaheim, or Sonora varieties because I can use a lot and get a big burst of flavor without actually blasting off. I wondered, however, about the toast-soak-and-pass method that is commonly recommended for preparing dried chilies—so much of the precious stuff ends up stuck in the strainer. There is flavor in those skins—why do we have to discard them?

So I started drying the dried chilies further, until they were brittle but not at all burned, and then grinding them to powder in a blender or spice mill. In order for you to do this, they do need to be completely crackly—bendy, leathery chilies won't grind. If your oven has a pilot light, then it's easy: spread them on a tray tonight, pop them in the unlit oven, and tomorrow morning they'll be ready for grinding. No pilot? Heat the oven to 250°F, turn it off, put the tray of chilies in, leave the door open for half a minute, then close it and wait an hour. Once they're dried, crack off the stem ends and shake the seeds out, then grind the chilies in your blender or a clean spice mill. (Electric spice mills can be cleaned by grinding a little handful of rice. If the mill was used for coffee, you may have to do it twice.)

Harissa keeps well, surface covered with a film of oil and refrigerated, for at least a week, and with that in mind, note that doubling this recipe can be an act of impressive resourcefulness.

Makes 1 cup and 1 stained shirt

2 tablespoons currants or raisins (optional)

¼ cup mild chili powder (about 8 whole chilies or a scant 2 ounces)

1 garlic clove, pounded with a pinch of salt

⅓ cup good olive oil

1 teaspoon red wine vinegar

Salt

Plump the currants or raisins, if using, in a small bowl with enough hot water to cover by ½ inch. If you're using raisins, chop them a little. Set them aside.

Put the chili powder in another small mixing bowl, add ⅜ cup hot water, stir, and set the mixture aside for 30 minutes to hydrate and become a paste. Stir the garlic paste, oil, red wine vinegar, and ¼ teaspoon salt into the chili paste. Drain the currants and stir them into the harissa. Taste and adjust. Since the texture and heat level can vary from individual chili to chili, you may want to add more oil if the harissa is too hot, water if it's too thick, or something spicy like cayenne if it's too meek.

Harissa gives a glow to couscous dishes and can be stirred into the broth before serving or passed at the table.

* *All grilled meats welcome harissa, especially lamb.*
* *For a breakfast with real fortitude, I like harissa with eggs boiled, poached, or fried.*
* *Chickpeas, lentils, or any bowl of beans is bettered with a big spoonful.*
* *If good dried chilies are just unavailable, or you can't be bothered with all the drying and grinding business, buy sambal oelek at an Asian market and make a quick, tasty harissa by stirring 3 tablespoons of it with 1 or more pounded garlic cloves and 5 tablespoons olive oil.*

FRESH TURMERIC SALSA

The wonderful Niloufer Ichaporia King brings her exotic food and saffron-colored magic to Chez Panisse every year to celebrate Navroz, the Parsi New Year. One spring, she showed us the basics of this salsa: fresh turmeric, salt, and lime juice. She slices the raw, bright orange rhizomes into thin fragrant coins, leaving golden patches on our cutting boards that linger for days, and tosses them with lime and salt, ginger, and green chilies. When Niloufer serves this salsa on toast with goat's-milk cheese, she calls it Krishna's breakfast, named after not the god but a friend of hers who enjoys it with his morning tea. I was instantly hooked and now make it often, sometimes putting some or all of it in a blender or mortar when I want it a little juicier, and sometimes adding crushed coriander seeds (the otherworldly fresh green ones are especially good, if you can find or grow them), pounded garlic, basil, or mint.

Makes about ½ cup

5 fresh turmeric fingers (about 3 ounces)

2 teaspoons minced or grated ginger (about 1 inch)

1 green chili, such as a serrano or jalapeño, seeded and diced tiny

½ teaspoon salt

Juice of 1 or 2 limes

Good olive oil, if needed

Sugar, if needed

Peel the turmeric and use a sharp knife to slice it in half lengthwise, and then across in very thin half moons. Mix the turmeric slices with the ginger, green chili, and salt, and squeeze in one or both limes, depending on how juicy they are. Stir well and allow the mixture to marinate for 30 minutes, then taste and adjust. If the turmeric is too intense or is bitter, I will sometimes add a teaspoon of oil, sugar, or both. Will keep, covered and refrigerated, for days.

* *Turmeric salsa has a dark earth/bright sun flavor combination that is nearly medicinal but in a good and, to me, addictive way. I like it with eggs or fish cooked any way, with grilled chicken or lamb, or, Krishna-like, on toast with soft cheese.*

MAYONNAISE, AÏOLI, AND ROUILLE

A simple mixture of eggs and oil that's infinitely variable, mayonnaise is often badly misrepresented, but when done right, will make a cook proud.

Makes 1 cup

1 egg yolk

1 teaspoon Dijon mustard

Salt

1 cup light olive oil (spicy olive oil can make mayonnaise bitter)

1 teaspoon red wine vinegar

1 teaspoon lemon juice

Whisk the egg yolk, mustard, and a pinch of salt together in a small bowl. The size matters here: the oil whisks into the egg yolk more readily in a snug vessel. It doesn't make sense, but somehow a mortar and pestle also works. Begin to add the oil drop by drop, stirring all the while. Drip slowly and stir quickly until the yolk begins to hold the oil and thicken, about a quarter of the way through. Now you can pour the oil in a little quicker, in a stream, but you cannot stop stirring. Find a friend if you're getting tired. Keep going and at about the ½-cup mark, the emulsion tends to get a little too thick, so add 1 teaspoon water. Use all the oil, and then stir in the vinegar and lemon juice. If the mayonnaise looks very shiny and bouncy, add drops of water to smooth it out. Taste and adjust.

* *Finely chop or pound herbs in a mortar, or puree in a blender, add some of the oil to the herbs, and then stir them into the mayonnaise. Mayonnaise with parsley, basil, chervil, or chives is great with fish, boiled vegetables, fried anything, hard-boiled eggs, roasted beets, or on a sandwich.*
* *To make tartar sauce, finely dice some shallots or slice some scallions and set them aside dressed with a little salt, lemon juice, or vinegar. Chop parsley and chives, chervil, or tarragon, and any combination of capers, cornichons, celery hearts, or hard-boiled eggs and stir them into the mayonnaise. Add 1 teaspoon mustard, a pinch of cayenne, and the shallots or scallions.*

Aïoli

Replace the mustard with 1 or more garlic cloves pounded with a little salt.
Some prefer aïoli with less, or zero, vinegar or lemon juice . . . Do some tasting
and decide for yourself.

Rouille

To make rouille, flavor aïoli with roasted pepper puree or sweet chili paste, or
both. For roasted pepper puree, set a whole red bell pepper, as is, atop a gas
burner turned up high. As each side chars, use tongs to turn to the next side
until the skin is blackened all over. Put the pepper in a bag or covered container and set it aside to steam. When cool, peel the charred skin off with your
fingers, pull off the stem end, and remove the seeds and membranes. Give the
pepper a quick rinse and put it in the blender with 1 teaspoon red wine vinegar
and a scant ¼ teaspoon salt. Puree until smooth, adding tablespoons of water
or oil if needed to get it going. For mild dried chili paste, see page 261. Whisk
a couple of tablespoons each of chili paste and roasted pepper puree into a batch
of aïoli *et voilà*: rouille. Make it a little spicy with cayenne if you like.

MOSTARDA

Somewhere between savory relish and fruit preserve with a mustardy mule kick, mostarda looks pretty but can blast out the sinuses, wasabi-style, if over-eaten. Traditional alongside brothy braises, mostardo also sparkles with grilled or roasted meats, and with fresh cheeses as well.

Makes about 1 quart

2 teaspoons fennel seeds

2 teaspoons coriander seeds

6 whole cloves

4 allspice berries

3 bay leaves

2 tablespoons mustard seeds

Crushed red pepper flakes

1 cup sugar

1 tablespoon red wine vinegar

1 pound Fuyu persimmons, cored, peeled, and cut into ¼-inch slices

½ pound figs, stemmed and cut into quarters

Mustard oil (findable at Indian or Asian markets, or online)

Toast the fennel, coriander, cloves, and allspice berries in a dry skillet and grind them to a powder with one of the bay leaves (page 9). Put the ground spices, remaining bay leaves, mustard seeds, red pepper flakes, and sugar in a saucepan with 2 cups of water and the vinegar. Bring the mixture to a boil, reduce it to a slow simmer, and cook for 10 minutes. Add the persimmons and figs, stir, and turn them out into a bowl to cool at room temperature. When cool, stir in the mustard oil, starting with just ½ teaspoon, tasting and adding more as you like.

* *Instead of persimmons and figs, use firm pears or peaches; chunky, green, unripe tomato and red pepper dice; roasted slices of Delicata or butternut squash; dried apricots and raisins . . .*
* *Mince or puree some or all of the mostarda if you want it saucier.*

SUMMER MARINARA

I am crazy for basil, and if I can't have pesto (because I've overdone it again and my son Liam can't take it anymore), then I want tomato sauce with really a lot of basil (which I'm pretty sure annoys him, too). The trick to this simple sauce is frying the basil leaves a little, like sautéing spinach—it sets the color and spreads the flavor through the oil and into the sauce.

Makes about 2½ cups, enough for lasagna (page 144) or to toss with spaghetti for 6

2 or 3 of the best large ripe tomatoes

Salt

¼ cup olive oil, plus more as needed

2 garlic cloves, very thinly sliced

1 bunch basil, leaves only, very roughly chopped

Bring a pot of water to a boil and slip the tomatoes in. Fish them out when the skins feel loose, around 30 seconds, and drop them into a bowl of ice water. When they're cool, use a paring knife to cut out the green stem ends and pull off the skins. If the skin is very stuck, drop the tomato back into the pot for a few seconds more. Cut the tomatoes in half at their equators and gently squeeze them, cut sides facing down, to get the seeds out. Cut the halves into dice. To draw out some liquid and intensify the flavor, put the diced tomatoes in a colander, sprinkle them with the salt, and let them sit for 10 minutes.

Heat a skillet to low and add the oil, then the garlic. Stir a bit until it sizzles, then add the basil and a sprinkle of salt. Raise the heat and cook the basil, stirring, until it's wilted and dark green, watching that you don't burn the garlic. Add the tomatoes and cook until they just lose their rawness, about 5 minutes. Taste and adjust.

* *Spoon over grilled or toasted thick slices of bread, make pizza (page 21), or use to top grilled steaks or chicken* alla pizzaiola.

PICKLED PEACHES AND RED ONIONS

Underripe fruit works best for this pickle. I suppose it's more condiment than sauce, and though I would not put it on a hot dog or burger, it could be very nice tucked in a roll with a sausage or slotted into a ham sammy with dabs of mustard. More often, I serve it with roasted or grilled pork, duck, or chicken, either as is in slices or chopped like a relish.

Makes 1 generous, picnicky quart

½ cup vinegar (white wine, cider, or red wine)

½ cup white wine

2 teaspoons salt

1 tablespoon sugar

2 bay leaves

1 teaspoon each coriander seeds, fennel seeds, mustard seeds

½ teaspoon black peppercorns

2 whole cloves

3 allspice berries

1½ pounds firm, underripe peaches

1 red onion

Combine all the ingredients except the peaches and onion in a medium saucepan with 4 cups water and bring the mixture to a boil over high heat. Lower the heat and simmer for 10 minutes. Meanwhile, using a vegetable peeler, peel the peaches, cut them into thin wedges, and set them aside in a mixing bowl.

Peel and cut the red onion into similar-size wedges or slices. Taste the brine and see if you want to add more sugar, salt, or spice. If it tastes too acid, add water. When it's right, add the onion, bring the liquid back to a boil, and pour the onion and brine over the peaches. Poke any exposed peach or onion under the brine and let the pickles cool at room temperature. Good right away, better the next day and for at least a week, if refrigerated.

* *Pickle plums, cherries, or apricots along with, or in place of, the peaches.*

SALSA DI NOCI

I first made this salsa to go with big greens-filled pasta called pansotti (page 121), but since it is really just a nuttier version of pesto, it works anywhere pesto would—tossed with spaghetti or hand-cut egg pasta (page 146), spooned over sliced tomatoes or grilled vegetables, and so on. I always make salsa di noci in a mortar, adding and pestling ingredients as I go, but you can also chop everything separately and then mix them together in a bowl.

Makes 1 overflowing cup

1 garlic clove

½ teaspoon salt

1 tablespoon chopped marjoram

¼ cup chopped parsley

⅓ cup toasted walnuts (see page 9)

¼ cup toasted pine nuts

¼ cup grated pecorino or Parmesan

½ cup salad olive oil

Add the ingredients, one by one, to the mortar, pounding through the garlic, salt, herbs, and nuts, and stirring in the cheese and oil. Or, pound only the garlic and salt, chop the nuts finely, and stir everything together in a bowl. Taste and adjust.

FINALLY:
DESSERTS

We were married, Kathleen and I, in early January, on the windy Connecticut coast, in a town we chose only because it was midway between the homes of my parents and hers. Though there had been a deep snowfall the night before, our wedding day was clear and, in white, the beach and my bride were very beautiful. It had been a cold winter, and we'd spent it, and much of the previous year, apartment-hopping around New York. Public school substitute teachers by day and waiters by night, we were solvent but itinerant—artists dreaming big in an expensive city. We stayed at some swell places: lofts in Tribeca and SoHo, an Upper East Side brownstone, a Jersey City floor-through with wide pumpkin-pine floorboards and sunny roof access, but we were ready to move on and get out, so we took ourselves on a long honeymoon—a month after our wedding, gifts cashed and paintbrushes packed, we flew to Italy to join friends at a farmhouse in the hills of Lucca. The winter is milder there and, above the stable, our rooms were warmed by the horses below after the Tuscan sun had set. But the stone walls were thick, and soon nights turned chilly, so we lit fires and sat around, finishing our wine and eating the blood oranges that were for sale in markets and by vendors along the road. Cutting through the sunset-colored skin and finding red flesh and juice was a sweet surprise every time, and soon we were hooked, feeding on the oranges at night like fruit bats, citrus vampires. We began to buy them by the case, and our friend Gianno taught us how to roll their crinkly, colorful papers into tubes, set the tubes upright in the hearth, and touch their edges with a match. The papers would rise, floating like lit leaves, drifting and dreamy in the smoky draft, and then shoot like rockets up through the flue.

Thousands of miles away and a lifetime later, we have our own fireplace, Kathleen and I, though not the rustic Tuscan farmhouse kitchen sort so good for launching paper rockets. We have work and family now, too, some projects smoldering, others alight—stuff more serious than sending orange wrappers flaming into the night. We still like to sit, though, after dinner with wine to finish, and eat oranges together. Proof, perhaps, that fruit is not only the best dessert but the food of love.

If, knowing that, one craves further confection to finish a meal on an especially gracious note, I offer these recipes.

Spring

RHUBARB FLAKY TART

The final course of the twentyish-course modern meal I was once served was a sort of landscape of ranging rhubarb iterations on a vast plate set atop a very slowly deflating linen pillow full of, and occasionally emitting, lavender smoke. An oddly melancholy culinary elegy and not something I expect *I'll* ever see again, let alone emulate, but I do love rhubarb. I have ever since I was a grubby kid bothering the old guy who used to come and fish in the pond near our house, asking him every kind of question fish, worm, or guts related. He'd sit on an upturned joint compound bucket, with another one for his gear, and a third for keepers. Mostly he caught bony, colorful sunfish—not keepers—and threw them onto the weedy banks, where they'd flop until skinny feral cats would swirl in, yowling and crunching. He was angling for big fish, bass that were said to swim deeper, if you could get past the sunnies. Even to me, this sounds made up, but I swear his name was Captain Charlie, or we called him that, anyway, and he brought us rhubarb, huge green and red stalks, fragrant from his garden in the spring. My mother would make pies, with strawberries, that still melt my heart like a scoop of vanilla.

I also love rhubarb stewed in chunks, soft and tender in simple syrup as I had it at an Irish bed and breakfast, or raw and crisp, sliced thin with mint and rocket, for a bracing salad, or made into an exotic salsa with cumin and scallions for grilled lamb or fish.

Or in this flaky tart.

Makes 1 tart to serve 8 to 10

1½ pounds rhubarb stalks, trimmed of leaf bits and tough ends and cut into 4-inch segments

¾ cup plus 2 tablespoons sugar

Grated zest from ½ orange

2 tablespoons all-purpose flour

1 rolled-out round of flaky tart dough (page 56)

1 egg or 2 tablespoons cream or melted, but not hot, butter

Cut the rhubarb segments lengthwise into ¼-inch strips and toss them in a bowl with ¾ cup of the sugar, the orange zest, and the flour. Stir to coat well.

Lay the tart round on a baking sheet and top it with the rhubarb mixture, leaving at least a 2-inch border. Arrange the rhubarb in a pattern, or no pattern—it will be overlapping and piled up and that's good. It should be a little deeper around the edges and shallower in the center. Fold the border up and over the rhubarb—not over all of it, just a frame around the edge, leaving the center uncovered. I go for random folds, but regular pleats could be nice. Brush the border with the egg, cream, or melted butter and sprinkle it generously with the remaining 2 tablespoons sugar. Avoid getting a lot of sugar on the baking sheet, and brush away any that does—it will burn.

Bake until the rhubarb is tender, the pastry border is caramel brown, and a peek underneath reveals the bottom to be browned and crisp as well, about 45 minutes. Let the tart sit for 5 minutes, then cut it and eat it warm or let it cool and eat it at room temperature a little later. Don't try to reheat the tart; it will get soggy.

* *Serve with lightly sweetened whipped cream or crème fraîche (page 248) or a combination of the two. Or with vanilla ice cream (page 278).*

VANILLA ICE CREAM, QUICK-STYLE

Having long tried and failed to muster the necessary courage to properly cook the eggy custard base called for in ice-cream-making, I've turned to this egg-less recipe. It is simple, virtually failure-proof, and really very good, especially if eaten immediately after churning.

Makes 1 quart

½ vanilla bean

3 cups cream

1 cup milk

1 cup sugar

½ teaspoon salt

Split the half vanilla bean in half lengthwise and scrape out the seeds with the edge of a knife. Put it all, scraped pod and scrapings, in a saucepan with 1 cup of the cream, the milk, sugar, and salt and stir over medium heat until the sugar is dissolved and the mixture is hot. Pour it into a bowl, stir in the remaining 2 cups cream, and refrigerate until completely chilled. Freeze in an ice cream maker according to the manufacturer's instructions.

APRICOT ICE CREAM

A ripe apricot is a blessed thing, when the flavor is sweet and especially when the texture is right. If you have a few, eat them right away, preferably before they've even been refrigerated. If you have a lot of them, or if the texture is less than ideal, apricots make great ice cream.

Makes 1 quart

1 pound ripe apricots (Royal Blenheims, Robadas, and Honey Rich are some favorites)

¾ cup sugar

¼ teaspoon salt

2 cups heavy cream

1 cup milk

With a vegetable peeler, peel the apricots, then cut out the pits. In a medium saucepan over medium heat, combine them with the sugar and salt and cook, crushing and mashing them with a potato masher or the back of a spoon, until they begin to get juicy. Turn the heat to low and cook until they are jammy, about 10 minutes. Pass the apricots through a food mill or whiz them in a food processor, let them cool, and mix them well with the cream and milk. Cover tightly and refrigerate the mixture until it is well chilled, a few hours or overnight.

Pour the mixture into your ice cream maker and freeze it according to the manufacturer's instructions.

* *Great with berries of any sort.*

MINT ICE MILK

My mom used to keep a carton of Sealtest ice milk in the freezer. Of course, we kids were hounds for sweets, but ice milk was a diet thing and so invisible to us. Mom was glad, I guess, but now I know that we really missed out: somewhere between sherbet and ice cream, ice milk is light and refreshing, and this version is like a fluffy cloud full of minty snow.

Makes 1 quart

1 quart milk

1 cup sugar

¼ teaspoon salt

Leaves from 10 mint sprigs
(about 1 cup)

4 egg whites

¼ teaspoon cream of tartar

Combine the milk, ½ cup of the sugar, and the salt in a medium saucepan over medium-high heat, stirring to dissolve the sugar. Bring just to a boil and then lower to a simmer. Roughly chop a third of the mint leaves and drop them into the milk. Steep for 90 seconds, then dip them out and repeat with the remaining leaves in two batches. Strain and chill completely. Discard the mint leaves.

In a mixing bowl, preferably a copper one, whisk the egg whites to froth, add the cream of tartar and 1 tablespoon sugar, and continue whisking, adding the rest of the sugar, 1 tablespoon at a time, as it is incorporated. When the meringue is shiny and just holds soft peaks (and your arm is tired, unless you're using an electric mixer), stir it into the minty milk.

Pour the mixture into your ice cream maker and freeze it according to the manufacturer's instructions. Eat it right away or if you freeze it for later, let it soften in the refrigerator for 30 to 45 minutes before scooping.

* *Serve with strawberries, hulled and quartered and tossed with a little sugar and some torn mint leaves.*

Summer

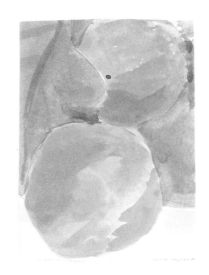

PEACHES

There is no way to improve upon a fat ripe peach in summer, eaten out of hand, all fuzz and juice. That's just a given, but for table use, a few things can and arguably should be done. Ripeness established, dunking a freestone peach into boiling water for 10 to 15 seconds, and immediately then into ice water, will allow the skin to slip off, as a tomato's will when given the same treatment. Remove the pit by cutting the fruit around, from pole to pole, and giving the halves a twist—if you're lucky it will come cleanly apart. If not, pry apart as you must to make it two. Slip them into a bowl of cool to cold simple syrup (recipe follows) for a couple of minutes or hours. You can chill them, if it's a hot day, but not so much as to cool their ardency. For serving, lift them out of the syrup into small bowls (if you have access to any sort of fruit tree leaves, peach or fig, set them in the bowls first), cut side up, and dollop whipped cream, sweetened lightly, vanilla extract optional, into the pit divot. Crème fraîche (page 248) can be nice in with the cream; yogurt, drained if there's time, does well, too. Fresh raspberry ice cream, or any other berry ice cream, yours or bought, is inevitably delicious in the divot.

Simple Syrup

Makes about 2½ cups, enough for 6 peach halves

2 cups sugar
1½ cups water

Combine the sugar and water in a saucepan, bring the mixture to a boil, and simmer until the sugar is dissolved, about 3 minutes. Cool and refrigerate until you're ready to use it. Simple syrup keeps for months in the refrigerator.

PEACHES WITH CRISP STUFFING

Peeled and pitted peach halves can also be baked into individual little fruit crisps by replacing the pit with a mixture of butter, nuts, and flour. Proceed with whipped cream, crème fraîche (page 248), or ice cream as opposite.

Makes 6 servings

⅓ cup walnuts

½ cup plus 2 tablespoons all-purpose flour

2 tablespoons granulated sugar

2 tablespoons brown sugar, lightly packed

Pinch of ground cinnamon (optional)

¼ teaspoon salt

4½ tablespoons cool unsalted butter

3 peaches, peeled (or not), halved and pitted

Preheat the oven to 350°F. Spread the walnuts on a baking sheet and toast until they are lightly browned, 8 to 10 minutes. When they've cooled, rub them in a cloth to remove as much of the skins as you can, then chop them coarsely.

In a mixing bowl, combine the nuts, flour, granulated sugar, brown sugar, cinnamon (if you like), and salt. Dice the butter as best you can and use your fingers to rub it into the flour-nut mixture. You want it to have a moist, crumbly texture that clumps together some and holds its shape when squeezed.

Place a sixth of the topping in each of the peach divots, set in a snug baking dish so that they don't tip over, and bake until the peaches are cooked through and the topping is browned, 20 to 30 minutes.

TENDER BERRY BUTTER TART

Pastry chefs Lindsey Shere and Mary Jo Thoresen go way back in the Chez Panisse family. This pairing of Lindsey's super-tender crust and Mary Jo's butter-cloud batter combines their geniuses and highlights our shared respect for berries, and all fruits. Knowing when to get out of the way of a perfectly ripe fruit in season is a skill that is all too rare, and these two women are masters. They know that if you are going to cook the ripest, sweetest raspberries, blackberries, or boysenberries of summer (which are not berries at all but *aggregates of drupelets*! Who knew?), when eating them raw out of hand is a hard-to-beat joy, the result sure better be at least as good. This tart passes the test with extra credit.

Makes one 9-inch tart

1 egg

¼ cup sugar

5 tablespoons butter

1 tablespoon plus 1 teaspoon all-purpose flour

Juice of ¼ lemon

Pinch of salt

½ teaspoon pure vanilla extract or 2 teaspoons fruit eau-de-vie or brandy (optional)

1 generous pint raspberries or similar berries like boysen- or black-

1 short tart shell, baked (recipe follows)

Heat the oven to 325°F.

In a large bowl, with a whisk or electric mixer, beat the egg with the sugar until the mixture turns pale and thickens enough to form a ribbon when you lift the whisk. It does take a while. Melt the butter in a little saucepan over medium heat and when it is bubbling hot, whisk it gradually into the egg and sugar mixture. Mix in the flour, lemon juice, salt, and vanilla or booze, if using, and stir just until completely incorporated. Spread the berries in the tart shell and

pour the batter evenly on top. Bake until slightly puffed and nicely browned, about 50 minutes. Let sit for 5 minutes before serving.

Short Tart Shell

The trick of making this dough is mixing the butter quickly and thoroughly with the flour so that it becomes the consistency of bread crumbs. If the butter starts too soft, or gets too soft from overhandling, the dough may become tough.

Makes one 9-inch tart shell

1 cup all-purpose flour

1 tablespoon sugar

¼ teaspoon salt

¼ teaspoon grated lemon zest

8 tablespoons (1 stick) unsalted
butter, frozen for at least
45 minutes

½ teaspoon pure vanilla extract

In a mixing bowl, combine the flour, sugar, salt, and lemon zest. Using the large holes of a box grater, grate the frozen butter into the flour mixture and toss with your fingers until the little bits of butter are all separate and not clumping. Set aside for 10 to 15 minutes, depending on your room's temperature, for the butter to defrost. With your fingertips, start crushing the butter bits as if you're making the gesture for lucre or trying to get its stain off your fingers. Don't use your whole hot hand: fingers only. When you don't see any more bits of butter and the mixture looks like fresh bread crumbs, add 1 tablespoon water and the vanilla and mix until the dough holds together when you squeeze it. Knead briefly, then shape it into a ball, flatten it into a disc, wrap it tightly, and chill it at least 30 minutes.

Let the dough come to cool room temperature, then press it with your fingers into a fluted tart pan with a removable bottom—this dough is too fragile for rolling out. Don't worry if it breaks apart, just keep going and it will come back together under your capable fingers. Be sure the dough fits into the corners of the pan and press around the sides and into the fluting. The dough should be of even thickness everywhere and can extend just above the sides of the pan top to allow for some shrinkage during baking.

Freeze the tart shell for 30 minutes, or for weeks if tightly wrapped, before baking. Heat the oven to 325°F and bake the tart shell until it's golden brown, 25 to 30 minutes.

PLUM FLAKY TART

When mangoes aren't my favorite fruit, plums are. This usually happens in early summer when a ripe rainbow of plums are on market tables, all sweetness and blush. Santa Rosa is the undisputed king of red plums; Emerald Beaut and Green Gage reign over the greens. Among the pluots, I like the aptly named Flavor King.

Makes one 13-inch tart

1½ pounds ripe plums

1 rolled-out round of flaky tart dough (page 56)

Scant tablespoon all-purpose flour, as needed

1 beaten egg or 2 tablespoons heavy cream or melted, but not hot, butter

About 2 tablespoons sugar

Heat the oven to 400°F.

Split the plums in half from top to bottom, cutting around the pit. Cut the halves into thin wedges that are about ¼ inch on the thick edge. Place the tart dough on a baking sheet and, if the plums seem very juicy, sprinkle flour to cover all but the outer 2 inches of the dough round.

Arrange the plum slices in a pattern, or no pattern, on the tart round, leaving at least a 2-inch border. The slices will be overlapping or piled up, and that's good—they should be a little deeper around the edges and shallower in the center. Fold the border up around the fruit—I go for random folds, but regular pleats could be nice. Brush the border with beaten egg, cream, or melted butter and sprinkle generously with the sugar. Avoid getting a lot of sugar on the baking sheet, and brush away any that does—it will burn.

Bake until the fruit is tender, the pastry border is caramel brown, and a peek underneath reveals the bottom to be browned and crisp as well, about

45 minutes. Let the tart sit for 5 minutes, then cut and eat it warm, or let it cool and eat it at room temperature a little later. Don't try to reheat the tart; it will get soggy.

* *Serve with lightly sweetened whipped cream or crème fraîche (page 248) or a combination of the two. Or with vanilla ice cream (page 278).*

FIG ICE CREAM

There used to be a fig tree by the garage across the street from our house in Oakland. The neighbors who parked their cars there saw it as nothing more than a nuisance, turning their driveway all jammy when the fruit fell, unappreciated, to the pavement. We were happy to help out, standing among the fragrant branches, avoiding bees, and picking the figs as they ripened. We'd eat our fill, give lots away, and then make this richly textured ice cream with the rest.

Makes 1 quart

1 basket fresh ripe figs (about 12 ounces; I like Black Mission or Adriatic), stemmed and cut into quarters

¾ cup sugar

¼ teaspoon salt

2 cups cream

1 cup milk

¼ cup plain whole milk yogurt

In a medium saucepan over medium heat, cook the figs, sugar, and salt, crushing and mashing the figs with a potato masher or the back of a spoon until they begin to get juicy. Turn the heat to low and cook until the mixture gets jammy, about 10 minutes. Pass the figs through a food mill or whiz them in a food processor, let them cool, and mix them well with the cream and milk. Cover tightly and refrigerate the mixture until well chilled, a few hours or overnight.

Stir in the yogurt for a little tanginess, then freeze the mixture in an ice cream maker according to the manufacturer's instructions.

* *Great with berries or roasted fig wedges, or alongside a slice of tart, or in a peach half (page 285).*

Fall

BOSC PEARS COOKED IN RED WINE

As a bonus to their rich burgundy color and pleasingly granular texture, these pears make the house smell really festive when you cook them with spices and red wine. Don't use your best, or worst, bottle for this recipe, of course. You can reuse the poaching liquid for up to a month.

Makes 6 servings

1 bottle red wine

1 cup sugar

½ vanilla bean, split lengthwise

Zest of ½ lemon, in strips

¼ stick cinnamon

12 black peppercorns

6 Bosc pears, just underripe, peeled, with stems left on

Combine all the ingredients except the pears in a pot deep enough to submerge the pears, add 1½ cups water, and bring the liquid to a boil over high heat. Turn the heat down to a simmer and cook for 15 minutes. Add the pears and use a saucer to weigh them down so that they're all below the surface. Cook until a paring knife blade meets very little resistance when inserted, about 1 hour. You can lift the pears from the wine and eat them as soon as they cool, but they are better left to soak in the refrigerator overnight, or for several days, and then brought to room temperature. Serve them with a spoonful of the poaching liquid. If you want a more syrupy sauce, reduce 1 cup of the liquid by half or more, then spoon it over the pear. Terribly good with crème fraîche ice cream (page 298).

* *Slice red-wine-cooked pears and use to replace up to half of the raw pears in a pear tart (page 299).*

CRÈME FRAÎCHE ICE CREAM, QUICK-STYLE

With a touch of tanginess to temper its richness, crème fraîche ice cream is like, but more elegant than, frogurt. A low elegance-bar to set, perhaps, but still.

Makes 1 quart

2 cups heavy cream

1 cup milk

1 cup sugar

½ teaspoon salt

1 cup crème fraîche (page 248)

In a medium saucepan, combine 1 cup of the cream, the milk, sugar, and salt and stir over medium heat until the sugar is dissolved. Pour the mixture into a bowl, stir in the remaining 1 cup cream and the crème fraîche, and refrigerate until it is completely chilled. Freeze in an ice cream maker according to the manufacturer's instructions.

PEAR FLAKY TART

We had three pear trees among the brambles bordering the yard of my child-hood home. They produced a lot of fruit, and I eagerly tasted it year after year but, sadly, the pears were always inedibly mealy. Or that's what I thought until a few years ago when I learned that pears must ripen *off* the tree—if you wait until they're soft to pick them, it's too late. Oh, the tragedy of the misspent fruits of my youth!

Makes one 13-inch tart

1½ pounds ripe pears (Warren are wonderful, as are Bartlett, Comice, and Anjou)

1 rolled-out round of flaky tart dough (page 56)

1 beaten egg or 2 tablespoons heavy cream or melted, but not hot, butter

About 2 tablespoons sugar

Heat the oven to 400°F. Using a Y-shaped vegetable peeler, peel the pears. Arrange the slices on the tart round, leaving at least a 2-inch border. The slices will be overlapping or piled up, and that's good—they should be a little deeper around the edges and shallower in the center. Fold the border up around the fruit—I go for random folds, but regular pleats could be nice. Brush the border with beaten egg, cream, or melted butter, and sprinkle generously with sugar. Avoid getting a lot of sugar on the baking sheet, and brush away any that does—it will burn. Bake until the fruit is tender, the pastry border is caramel brown, and a peek underneath reveals the bottom to be browned and crisp as well, about 45 minutes. Let the tart sit for 5 minutes before cutting and eating it warm, or let it cool and eat it at room temperature a little later. Don't try to reheat the tart; it will get soggy.

* *Serve with lightly sweetened whipped cream or crème fraîche (page 248) or a combination of the two. Or with vanilla ice cream (page 278).*
* *Replace up to half of the pear with sliced pears poached in red wine (page 297).*

PERSIMMON TOAST WITH CHOCOLATE, PISTACHIOS, AND CREAM

Hachiya persimmons, the kind that sting and spite if bitten before ready, but when ripe, yield themselves up, flesh quivering at the tenderest caresses, are among the sexiest of fruits. They are so luscious that eating one can be almost too sensual to do in public—lips smack, juices gush, slurping happens. Contrasting their softness with crunch, their sweetness with bitter, I came up with this easy dessert. It's simple, so use best-quality ingredients—nice bread, excellent bitter chocolate, and persimmons so ripe it verges on embarrassing.

Makes 6 servings

1 cup heavy cream or a combination of half heavy cream, half crème fraîche (page 248)

1 teaspoon sugar

6 half slices rustic bread

Soft unsalted butter

2 to 3 ounces bittersweet chocolate

Salt

3 ripe Hachiya persimmons

⅓ cup pistachios, toasted and chopped (see page 9)

Whip the cream with the sugar to soft peaks and set aside.

Toast the bread in a 425°F oven or in a toaster until browned and crunchy outside, soft inside. While the toast is still hot, butter it quickly, then grate on the chocolate and sprinkle lightly with salt. Cut the persimmons in half, top to bottom, and scoop the flesh out from the skin and onto the toasts, one half per. Dollop each with whipped cream, sprinkle with pistachios, and serve.

POMEGRANATE ICE WITH GOLDEN ALMOND TUILES

There is a lesson to be learned about pleasure from watching a kid eat a pomegranate. The joy seems to lie in the puzzle-disassembling aspect of it, a curiously solid yet fragile little puzzle made of clear bubbles of ruby juice that stack up together, squaring each other off and leaving patterned divots in their chalky white and red shell. The bubbles are firm, but snap easily between the teeth with little bursts of sweet-tart liquid and a flinty kernel crunch. And they just keep coming, like a carload of tiny crimson clowns squirting juice and spreading red smiles. This mythic fruit offers a choice between gratifications realized or delayed as well: as with any food that must be hand harvested—nutmeats, crabmeat, berries—a decision must be made to either eat the sweet seeds as you pick, or pick, pile, and then eat.

A pomegranate, I say, in every lunch box!

Makes 6 servings

1 quart cold, unsweetened pomegranate juice (best you can get and preferably organic and fresh; from concentrate works in a pinch)

Juice of 2 limes

¾ cup plus 1 teaspoon sugar

1 cup heavy cream

½ cup pomegranate seeds

6 saffron and almond tuiles (recipe follows)

In a large bowl, combine the fruit juices and the ¾ cup sugar and whisk until the sugar is completely dissolved. Taste and adjust, remembering that sweet and sour flavors are dulled somewhat when frozen.

Ice cream machine method: Freeze the mixture in an ice cream machine, according to the manufacturer's instructions.

Food processor method: Pour the juice into ice cube trays or a flat pan and freeze it for at least 6 hours. Working in batches, grind the frozen juice in a food processor until fluffy and even textured. Keep the finished batches in a bowl in the freezer while you grind the rest.

Manual spoon-scraping method: Freeze the juice in a bowl until completely set, at least 12 hours. Use a large soupspoon to scrape up snowy shavings of the ice.

All methods, to finish: Whip the cream with the remaining 1 teaspoon sugar to soft peaks. Serve the ice in a glass, layered with dollops of whipped cream, sprinkled with pomegranate seeds, and with a saffron tuile cookie alongside.

Saffron and Almond Tuiles

This is a variation on a recipe I got from my friend Anthony, a culinary polymath who forages mushrooms and cooks everything from backyard wood-fired pizzas to sophisticated pastries with mastery. In these delicate tuile cookies, the saffron floats exotically along on the sweet orange and almond crispness.

Makes about 20 tuiles

¼ teaspoon saffron threads (10 to 12 threads)

8 tablespoons (1 stick) unsalted butter

⅜ cup strained orange juice

Grated zest of ½ orange

1¼ cups sugar

½ cup all-purpose flour

2 tablespoons black sesame seeds

1½ cups sliced almonds

Crush the saffron threads to a powder with the back of a spoon in a medium saucepan. Add the butter, juice, zest, and sugar to the pan and heat over medium, stirring until the butter is melted. Turn off the heat, add the flour, sesame seeds, and almonds, and stir well. Turn the dough out into a bowl, cover, and refrigerate till cool, at least 1 hour.

Heat the oven to 375°F and line a baking sheet with parchment paper.

Place teaspoonfuls of the dough on the prepared baking sheet, leaving plenty of room for spreading—you can fit 6 or 8 per sheet, depending on how big you make them. With damp fingers, flatten the spoonfuls into circles about 1 inch in diameter. Bake, rotating the sheet halfway through, until the tuiles are evenly browned, about 8 minutes. Let them cool for a minute, then use a spatula to move them to a platter while you bake more, if desired.

The dough keeps refrigerated for a week and frozen for months. If the weather is damp, keep the baked tuiles in a sealed container to maintain crispness.

MANGO FOOL

You may have your favorite fruits, but I think we can all agree . . . herald . . . with adulation . . . that the mango really is the best. I am a fool for mango because I love to eat them but also, and not least, because a mango's skin color manages to mix green and red and come up with orange, which is, according to the color wheel I made back in art school, impossible. A mango can further flip the world on its head by making us realize, in one bite, that the reason we like ripe fruits is not, as we so often claim to kids, because they taste as sweet as candy—no, we like candy, if we do, because it reminds us of ripe fruit. We take a bite and think, *Oh, this is what Skittles* (or whatever) *are supposed to taste like. Dang, they got that wrong!* If further convincing of the mango's superiority is required, one need look no further than the brilliant and popular porcupine technique—slash-and-invert—for eating this tropical prince of fruits.

Makes 6 servings

2 large ripe mangoes

2 limes

1 tablespoon plus 1½ teaspoons sugar

1 cup heavy cream

¾ cup coconut milk

½ cup toasted coconut

Chill six glasses to layer the fool into. Stemmed glasses are nice.

With a vegetable peeler, peel the mangoes and, carefully—peeled mangoes are very slippery—cut 2 large side fillets from the pit of each mango. Cut what you can from the edges as well, so that you end up with 4 large fillets and 4 edge pieces. Chew on one of the pits and give the other to a friend. Save the 2 nicest-looking big fillets for slicing and cut the others, along with the edge pieces, into chunks for the blender. Whiz them smooth with the juice of 1½ limes and 1 tablespoon of the sugar and refrigerate the puree until cold.

Cut the reserved pretty mango fillets lengthwise into long ¼-inch slices. Squeeze the remaining half lime over them and sprinkle with ½ teaspoon of the sugar, just to give them some shine. Toss them gently to coat and set them aside.

In a large bowl, combine the cream, coconut milk, and remaining 1 teaspoon sugar and whip to soft peaks.

Divide the mango slices among the glasses, sticking them to the insides so they stand vertically. Layer in the mango puree and the whipped cream so that it looks pretty from the side, like one of those childhood colored sand-scapes. Sprinkle the toasted coconut and pass the spoons.

Winter

CHOCOLATE ICE WITH CRISP ALMOND MERINGUES

I am into my third decade of son-raising, and if there's one thing I've learned, it's this: When you buy a kid a cup of hot cocoa, he will drink about half and then spill the rest. Sometimes not on you, but usually. This ice tastes like a frozen hot cocoa, oxymoronic as that may sound, and doesn't spill as easy.

Makes 6 servings

¾ cup plus 2 tablespoons plus 1 teaspoon sugar

½ cup unsweetened cocoa powder (quality cocoa, and chocolate, can make a big difference; I like Valrhona, Guittard, and TCHO)

¼ teaspoon salt

1 teaspoon pure vanilla extract

7 ounces bittersweet chocolate, chopped

1 cup heavy cream

6 crisp almond meringues (recipe follows)

Candied kumquat slices (page 313)

In a saucepan over high heat, bring 4 cups of water and the ¾ cup plus 2 tablespoons sugar to a boil, whisking once or twice to dissolve the sugar. Whisk in the cocoa powder and cook, simmering and stirring occasionally, for 5 minutes. Remove the pan from the heat, add the salt and vanilla, and set it aside to cool.

Meanwhile, melt the chocolate in a mixing bowl set over simmering water. When the cocoa mixture feels warm to the touch, but no longer hot, begin to whisk it into the melted chocolate, starting slowly and mixing completely with each addition. When it's all in, pass it through a strainer and refrigerate to chill completely, then freeze it in an ice cream maker according to the manufacturer's instructions. If you're not going to eat the ice right away, make sure to temper it in the refrigerator for 30 to 45 minutes before scooping.

Whip the cream with the remaining 1 teaspoon sugar, dollop it onto crisp meringues, top with a scoop of chocolate ice, and scatter candied kumquat slices on top.

Crisp Almond Meringues

Egg whites keep for weeks in the refrigerator, so save them when you use the yolks for mayonnaise or béarnaise and make meringues.

Makes about 24 meringues

2 egg whites

¼ teaspoon cream of tartar

½ cup sugar

⅛ teaspoon salt

½ teaspoon pure vanilla extract

3 tablespoons chopped toasted almonds (see page 9)

Heat the oven to 200°F and line a baking sheet with parchment paper.

In a mixing bowl, preferably a copper one, whisk the egg whites to froth, add the cream of tartar and 1 tablespoon of the sugar, and continue whisking, adding tablespoons of sugar. When all the sugar has been added and the meringue is shiny and holds firm peaks (and your arm is tired, unless you're using an electric mixer), stir in the salt, vanilla, and almonds.

Drop rounded tablespoonfuls on the prepared baking sheet and spread them into flat ovals about ½-inch thick. Bake until the meringues are completely dry and crisp, about 2 hours. Store them in an airtight container if you're not eating them right away.

Candied Kumquat Slices

Makes about 1 cup

¼ pound kumquats (about 10 pieces)
⅓ cup sugar

Cut the kumquats crosswise into ⅛-inch slices, discarding the ends and picking out seeds as you slice.

Combine the sugar with ⅓ cup water in a saucepan and bring the mixture to a boil over high heat, stirring to dissolve the sugar. Add the sliced kumquats, turn off the heat, and leave them to cool completely. Store the kumquats in the syrup, covered and refrigerated, until you're ready to serve. Will keep several weeks.

* *The extra syrup can be used to flavor bubbly things like water, prosecco, cava, or champagne.*

APPLE FLAKY TART WITH LEMON PEEL

Of course, apples are harvested in the fall and should be eaten and cooked then, but they store really well, and sometimes, in deep winter, before the citrus season has begun, they are the right fruit, especially for baking.

Makes one 13-inch tart

1½ pounds apples, Pink Lady, Sierra Beauty, or your favorite

5 tablespoons sugar, more as needed

1 tablespoon grated lemon zest, plus more as needed

1 rolled-out round of flaky tart dough (page 56)

1 beaten egg or 2 tablespoons heavy cream or melted, but not hot, butter

Heat the oven to 400°F.

Using a Y-shaped vegetable peeler, peel the apples. Put the peels in a saucepan with 2 tablespoons of the sugar and ¼ cup water. Bring the mixture to a boil, stirring occasionally, lower it to a slow simmer, and cook for 30 minutes, crushing the peels with the back of a spoon from time to time. Strain and reserve the liquid for painting the baked tart.

While the peels are cooking, quarter the apples. Use a paring knife to cut out the cores and stems, then cut the quarters into ⅛-inch slices. In a big bowl, toss the apple slices with 1 tablespoon of the sugar and the lemon zest. Taste a slice and add another tablespoon sugar and/or more zest if needed. Arrange the slices in a pattern, or no pattern, on the tart round, leaving at least a 2-inch border. The slices will be overlapping or piled up, and that's good—they should be a little deeper around the edges and shallower in the center. Fold the border up around the fruit—I go for random folds, but regular pleats could be nice. Brush the border with beaten egg, cream, or melted butter and sprinkle generously with sugar, about 2 tablespoons. Avoid getting a lot of sugar on the baking sheet, and brush away any that does—it will burn.

Bake until the fruit is tender, the pastry border is caramel brown, and a peek underneath reveals the bottom to be browned and crisp as well, about 45 minutes. Let the tart sit for 5 minutes, then use a brush to dab the apple slices with the reserved peel liquid for shine and juiciness. Eat it warm, or let it cool and eat it at room temperature a little later. Don't try to reheat the tart; it will get soggy.

Serve with lightly sweetened whipped cream or crème fraîche (page 248) or a combination of the two. Or with vanilla ice cream (page 278).

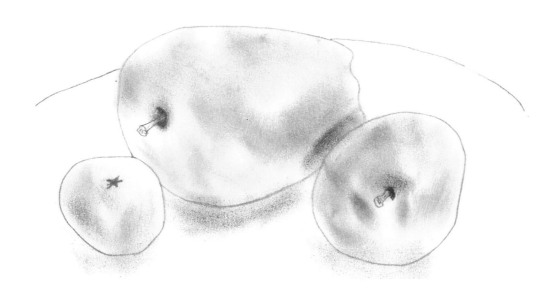

ORANGE AND CARDAMOM CREAM TART

Sometimes heavy cream can, counterintuitively, lighten. The filling for this tart displays that illogic by adding not-light whipped cream to not-light pastry cream and coming up yes-light. In feeling, anyway, and the bright fruit on top only furthers the freshness.

Makes one 9-inch tart

1 cup half-and-half

1 cardamom pod, crushed

4 tablespoons plus 1 teaspoon sugar

3 egg yolks

Pinch of salt

1½ tablespoons cornstarch

½ teaspoon pure vanilla extract

2 tablespoons cold unsalted butter, cut into 4 chunks

3 or 4 large oranges

¾ cup cream

1 baked sweet tart shell (recipe follows)

In a medium saucepan, combine the half-and-half, cardamom, and 3 tablespoons of the sugar and bring the mixture to a simmer over medium heat, stirring to dissolve the sugar.

Meanwhile, in a medium bowl, whisk the egg yolks with 1 tablespoon of the sugar and the salt until creamy, about 30 seconds. Add the cornstarch and vanilla and whisk another 45 seconds. Slowly whisk in one ladle of the hot half-and-half mixture to temper the eggs, then add another, and then the rest. Return the mixture to the saucepan and stir it with a rubber spatula over medium-low heat until it thickens to sour cream consistency. This won't take long, and if some curdling happens, don't worry; it will be resolved. Quickly add the chunks of cold butter, whisk until they're melted in, and then pour the mixture through a fine strainer to remove the cardamom and any lumps.

Place a piece of plastic wrap directly on top of the pastry cream to prevent a skin from forming and then refrigerate until it is completely cold, at least 3 hours.

Just before assembling the tart, use a sharp, narrow-bladed knife to cut slices from the top and bottom of an orange, as if you are lopping off the polar ice caps. Cut enough off so that you see a small circle of the flesh within. Set the orange on one of the flat ends and, in a motion that describes a curve, carve off a strip of skin just down to the flesh. Rotate the orange and repeat taking off strips until the orange is skinless. Trim off any pithy bits you may have missed. Holding the peeled orange in your palm, cut segments out from between the membranes, making clean little wedges, and set them aside.

When the pastry cream is cold, in a medium bowl, whip the cream with the remaining 1 teaspoon sugar to firm peaks. Add the pastry cream and keep whipping until the mixture is very thick and holds a shape. Spread it into the baked tart shell. Remove the fluted ring and cut the tart into wedges, then top it with the oranges so that they stay pretty and don't get pressed into the soft filling by the knife.

* *In other seasons, use other soft fruits such as mangoes, berries, or peaches.*
* *Leave out the cardamom or replace it with a few slices of raw ginger, ½ teaspoon anise seeds, or 1 star anise.*

Sweet Tart Shell

Makes one 9-inch tart shell

¼ cup sugar

1½ cups all-purpose flour

⅛ teaspoon salt

8 tablespoons (1 stick) butter, frozen for at least 45 minutes

1 egg yolk

2 tablespoons heavy cream, milk, or half-and-half

In a large bowl, sift together the sugar, flour, and salt. Using the large holes of a box grater, grate the frozen butter into the flour mixture and toss with your fingers until the little bits of butter are all separate and not clumping.

Set aside for 10 to 15 minutes, depending on your room's temperature, for the butter to defrost. With your fingertips, start crushing the butter bits, as if you're making the gesture for lucre or trying to get its stain off your fingers. Don't use your whole hot hand: fingers only. When you don't see any more bits of butter and the mixture looks like fresh bread crumbs, stir the yolk and cream together and add them to the dough, mixing with your hands until it comes together and can be formed into a ball. Knead briefly, then shape the dough into a ball, flatten it into a disc, wrap it tightly, and chill it for at least 30 minutes.

Let the dough come to cool room temperature and press it with your fingers into a fluted tart pan with a removable bottom—this dough is too fragile for rolling out. Don't worry if it breaks apart, just keep going, and it will come back together under your capable fingers. Be sure the dough fits into the corners of the pan; press it around the sides and into the fluting. The dough should be of even thickness everywhere and can extend just above the sides of the pan to allow for some shrinkage during baking.

Freeze the tart shell for 30 minutes, or for weeks if tightly wrapped, before baking.

Heat the oven to 325°F. Bake the tart shell until it is light golden brown, 25 to 30 minutes.

CHOCOLATE SOUFFLÉ

Making a soufflé might seem hard, but it's really not, and the result—a hot, fragrant, chocolaty magnificence—impresses. Even if it somehow gets under-baked (gooey), or overbaked (cakey), is that so bad? I like best to eat it with nothing more than cool cream poured over.

Makes 6 servings

Unsalted butter, at room temperature, to grease the baking dish

¼ cup sugar, plus more to coat the baking dish

8 ounces semisweet chocolate, chopped

¼ cup milk

1 teaspoon pure vanilla extract

4 eggs, separated

¼ teaspoon cream of tartar

Heat the oven to 350°F.

Use your fingers to liberally grease a soufflé dish or other straight-sided baking dish with butter. Add a spoonful of sugar and roll the dish around to coat. Tip out the excess sugar.

Melt the chocolate in a double boiler with the milk and vanilla. Stir until the mixture is melted and warm, but not hot, and then turn off the heat and stir in 3 of the egg yolks (save the fourth for . . . mayonnaise?).

In a mixing bowl, preferably a copper one, whisk the egg whites to froth, add the cream of tartar and 1 tablespoon sugar, and continue whisking, adding the sugar tablespoon by tablespoon. When all the remaining sugar has been added and the meringue is shiny and just holds soft peaks (and your arm is tired, unless you're using an electric mixer), fold the egg whites together with the chocolate mixture, stirring just until they are fully combined so as not to deflate the whites. Pour the mixture into the prepared dish and bake,

without opening the oven, for 25 minutes. Carefully check to see if the soufflé is set in the center—it should just jiggle a little. If it jiggles a lot, bake another 5 minutes. Eat right away while it's hot (though leftover soufflé is nearly as wonderful, it turns out, eaten straight out of the fridge).

ACKNOWLEDGMENTS

Thank you to:

Farmers and ranchers, for growing the food. You sustain us.

My wife and sons, for being everything to me and for making all this art.

My mom and dad and sister and brother, for your love, laughs, and support.

Tablemates who are hungry for art, music, literature, and good food. You make dinner so much more fun.

Alice Waters and all the members of the glorious and far-flung family of Chez Panisse, for cooking with me.

Carrie Lewis and Mary Jo Thoresen and all the pastry cooks, for your patient help and sweet advices. And Anthony Tassinello for tuiles.

Frances McDormand and Chris Thile, for their kind contributions.

Monterey Market, Magnani's Poultry, Monterey Fish Market, Kermit Lynch Wine Merchant, Acme Bread Company, Country Cheese Coffee Market, and Giovanni's Produce and Grocery, for the supplies.

Lori Wood and Kelly Sicat at Montalvo Center for the Arts, Lee Hudson and Cristina Salas-Porras Hudson at Hudson Ranch, and Fred Reid, for nice, quiet places to write.

Ed Anderson and George Dolese, for the pictures and plates.

Cassie Jones, for getting it so well.

Everyone at William Morrow, including Anna Brower, Suet Chong, Lynn Grady, Tavia Kowalchuk, Mumtaz Mustafa, Kate Schafer, Liate Stehlik, Rachel Meyers, and Kara Zauberman, for this book, and for the previous one. So very nicely done.

Sharon Bowers, for sage advice.

UNIVERSAL CONVERSION CHART

Oven temperature equivalents

250°F = 120°C   350°F = 180°C   450°F = 230°C

275°F = 135°C   375°F = 190°C   475°F = 240°C

300°F = 150°C   400°F = 200°C   500°F = 260°C

325°F = 160°C   425°F = 220°C

Measurement equivalents

Measurements should always be level unless directed otherwise.

⅛ teaspoon = 0.5 mL

¼ teaspoon = 1 mL

½ teaspoon = 2 mL

1 teaspoon = 5 mL

1 tablespoon = 3 teaspoons = ½ fluid ounce = 15 mL

2 tablespoons = ⅛ cup = 1 fluid ounce = 30 mL

4 tablespoons = ¼ cup = 2 fluid ounces = 60 mL

5⅓ tablespoons = ⅓ cup = 3 fluid ounces = 80 mL

8 tablespoons = ½ cup = 4 fluid ounces = 120 mL

10⅔ tablespoons = ⅔ cup = 5 fluid ounces = 160 mL

12 tablespoons = ¾ cup = 6 fluid ounces = 180 mL

16 tablespoons = 1 cup = 8 fluid ounces = 240 mL

INDEX

Note: Page references in *italics* indicate photographs.